TAIWAN

Travel Guide 2023

Discover The Hidden Gems of Taiwan: Ultimate Travel Guide

William J. Phillips

Table of Contents

Introduction.....5

Welcome to Taiwan.....11

History and Culture.....13

Weather and Climate.....18

Festival and Events.....24

Best Time to Visit.....31

Visa and Travel Documents.....36

Transportation.....43

Accommodation.....50

Traditional Taiwanese Cuisine.....54

Night market.....65

Bubble Tea.....75

Top Places to Visit in Taiwan.....81

Outdoor adventure in Taiwan.....113

Shopping in Taiwan.....117

Taiwanese Street Markets.....121

Useful Taiwan vocabulary and phrases.....123

Taiwan Dos and Don'ts.....128

15 Days Recommended Itineraries.....135

Conclusion 149

Introduction

I had always wanted to travel to Asia, and after much consideration, I decided that Taiwan would be the perfect destination for my next vacation. I had heard so much about the incredible food, breathtaking scenery, and the warmth of the Taiwanese people, and I couldn't wait to experience it all for myself.

I landed in Taipei, the bustling capital city, and was immediately struck by the vibrant energy of the place. I checked into my hotel, and after a quick rest, set out to explore the city. My first stop was Taipei 101, the world's tallest building. As I rode the elevator to the observation deck, I was amazed at the breathtaking views of the city below.

Next on my list was the National Palace Museum, which houses some of the most exquisite treasures of Chinese art and culture. As I wandered through the museum's halls, I was awed by the stunning jade carvings, intricate porcelain vases, and delicate silk scrolls. It was a true feast for the senses.

I also made sure to visit the famous Longshan Temple, a

historic Buddhist temple that dates back to the 18th century. As I watched the devoted worshippers offering incense and making offerings to the Buddha statues, I felt a deep sense of peace and tranquility.

After a few days in Taipei, I decided to venture out into the countryside to experience the natural beauty of Taiwan. My first stop was the stunning Taroko Gorge, a natural wonder of towering cliffs, cascading waterfalls, and crystal-clear streams. I spent the day hiking along the trails, breathing in the fresh mountain air and marveling at the incredible scenery.

From there, I traveled to Sun Moon Lake, a serene oasis in the heart of Taiwan. The lake's tranquil waters shimmered in the sunlight, and I spent my days lounging on the shore, reading a book and sipping on local tea.

No trip to Taiwan would be complete without sampling the incredible food, and I made sure to indulge in as many culinary delights as possible. From the night markets of Taipei, where I sampled everything from savory dumplings to sweet shaved ice, to the local seafood restaurants in the coastal town of Hualien, where I feasted on fresh fish and crab, every meal was a new adventure.

But the highlight of my culinary experiences in Taiwan was a visit to Din Tai Fung, the famous restaurant chain that originated in Taipei and is now beloved by foodies around the world for its steamed dumplings. As I bit into the juicy, savory dumplings filled with pork and crab, I knew that this was a taste that would stay with me forever.

As my vacation drew to a close, I reflected on my time in Taiwan and all that I had experienced. From the vibrant cities to the stunning natural beauty, from the rich cultural history to the incredible food, Taiwan truly had something for everyone. But what I would remember most was the warmth and generosity of the Taiwanese people, who had welcomed me with open arms and made me feel at home in their country.

I knew that I would return to Taiwan someday, to continue exploring all that this amazing place had to offer. And as I boarded my flight back home, I felt grateful for the memories I had made and the experiences I had shared with the people of Taiwan.

As I landed back home, I couldn't help but think about my next trip to Taiwan. The country had left an indelible mark on me, and I knew that I had to come back and explore more of its wonders.

I had been so captivated by the natural beauty of Taroko Gorge and Sun Moon Lake that I wanted to see more of Taiwan's landscapes. So, I started planning my next trip, and this time, I decided to focus on the eastern part of the island.

I started in Taitung, a charming coastal city that is known for its laid-back atmosphere and stunning beaches. I rented a scooter and set out to explore the surrounding countryside. I visited the picturesque Luye Highland, where I witnessed the annual hot air balloon festival and soared above the rolling hills and verdant rice paddies.

I also visited the nearby Sanxiantai, a scenic coastal area that boasts an iconic eight-arch bridge and a picturesque lighthouse. The rock formations and the crystal-clear water made it a perfect spot for snorkeling.

From Taitung, I headed to Hualien, a bustling city located on the east coast of Taiwan. Hualien is the gateway to Taroko Gorge, and I was eager to explore more of this stunning natural wonder.

I spent a few days hiking through the narrow canyon, marveling at the towering cliffs, the cascading waterfalls, and the crystal-clear streams. I also visited the nearby Qingshui Cliff, a breathtaking coastline with steep cliffs plunging into the Pacific Ocean.

But the highlight of my trip to Hualien was visiting the indigenous villages that are scattered throughout the surrounding mountains. I met the Amis, Atayal, and Bunun tribes, and learned about their customs, traditions, and way of life. I was struck by their kindness, generosity, and deep connection to the land.

As my trip came to an end, I realized that Taiwan was a country of many wonders, and that I had barely scratched the surface of all that it had to offer. I left knowing that I would return someday, to explore more of its natural beauty, learn more about its rich cultural heritage, and savor more of its delicious food.

But what had made my trip to Taiwan truly unforgettable was the warmth and kindness of its people. They had welcomed me with open arms, shared their stories and traditions, and made me feel like I was part of their community. It was this human connection that had made my trip so special, and that had left a lasting impression on me.

As I look back on my Taiwan vacation, I realize that it wasn't just a journey to a new country, but a journey of discovery and transformation. I had discovered new landscapes, new cultures, and new flavors, but I had also discovered something deeper within myself. I had learned that travel is not just about seeing new places, but about opening your heart and mind to new experiences, and connecting with the world in a profound way.

And so, I invite you to embark on your own journey to Taiwan, to discover its many wonders, and to experience the warmth and hospitality of its people. Whether you're seeking adventure, relaxation, or cultural immersion, Taiwan has something for everyone. So, pack your bags, and get ready for the trip of a lifetime. The Land of Treasures is waiting for you.

Welcome to Taiwan

Welcome to Taiwan, a dynamic and alluring place that skillfully combines traditional culture with cutting-edge innovation. Taiwan is a gem of East Asia that provides visitors a one-of-a-kind and amazing experience. It is nestled between the huge Pacific Ocean and the towering peaks of the Central Mountain Range.

You will experience the warm and welcoming friendliness of the island's residents from the time you land in Taiwan. Confucianism, Buddhism, Taoism, and other traditional ideas have a strong hold on the local culture, which is reflected in its art, architecture, and cuisine.

Ancient temples, soaring skyscrapers, and pulsating night markets coexist in harmony in Taiwan's cities, providing a look into the nation's rich and varied cultural legacy. The nation's capital, Taipei, is a hive of activity with a striking skyline, a thriving street food scene, and a number of top-notch museums and art galleries.

Taiwan is a treasure trove of natural beauties outside of the city limits, with beautiful scenery that includes rocky coasts, lush forests, and towering mountain ranges. By hiking, cycling, or just enjoying a leisurely stroll through one of Taiwan's several national parks, tourists may discover the island's natural splendor.

In addition, Taiwan is recognized for its delectable cuisine, which ranges from the well-known street cuisines of Taipei's night markets to the opulent flavors of the nation's best restaurants. The emphasis on fresh, in-season ingredients and robust, nuanced tastes that characterize Taiwanese cuisine, which is a combination of Chinese, Japanese, and indigenous influences.

Taiwan offers something to offer everyone, regardless of whether they are looking for adventure, relaxation, or cultural immersion. Therefore, visit Taiwan and discover for yourself why it is one of Asia's most enticing and magical destinations.

History and Culture

Taiwan, usually referred to as the Republic of China (ROC), is an East Asian island country. It is located north of the Philippines, south of Japan, and east of China. One of the world's most densely populated nations, Taiwan has a population of over 23 million. The island is renowned for its breathtaking landscapes, thriving cities, and extensive history and culture. I will go deeply into Taiwan's history and culture in this guide.

Taiwan's history goes back to the Stone Age. Aborigine tribes from Southeast Asia who spoke Austronesian were the first to settle on the island. The indigenous peoples of Taiwan, which are made up of these tribes, still make up about 2% of the country's total population.

Following the Spanish and Ming Dynasty supporters who fled to Taiwan after their rulers were overthrown in 1644, the Dutch built a trade base in Taiwan at the beginning of the 17th century. The Qing Dynasty invaded Taiwan in 1683 and held control of it until 1895.

Following the First Sino-Japanese War's defeat, the Qing Dynasty lost Taiwan to Japan in 1895 as part of the Treaty of Shimonoseki. Taiwan's culture, economy, and politics were significantly impacted by the 50-year Japanese colonial rule. Modern infrastructure and education were brought to Taiwan by the Japanese, who significantly changed the country. However, tyranny, forced labor, and cultural repression were also characteristics of Japanese colonial rule.

Taiwan was given back to Chinese control after Japan was defeated in World War II. Chiang Kai-shek's ROC government seized power in Taiwan and has remained in charge of the territory ever since. Since then, there has been debate over Taiwan's political status, with some nations acknowledging it as an independent nation and others viewing it as a province of China.

The culture of Taiwan is a distinctive fusion of indigenous, Chinese, and Japanese elements. Due to its strategic position at the crossroads of East Asia, Taiwan has been able to absorb cultural elements from many different nations and build its own unique culture.

Taiwanese cuisine is recognized for its variety and depth of taste. The most well-known Taiwanese foods include stinky tofu, oyster omelets, and beef noodle soup. Sushi and dumplings are only two examples of the various foods found in Taiwanese cuisine that have Chinese and Japanese influences.

Buddhism, Taoism, and Christianity are just a few of the many distinct religions that are practiced in Taiwan. Additionally, there are other traditional folk religions that have been practiced for generations in Taiwan. In Taiwanese society, religion is highly valued, and numerous festivals and celebrations are built on religious observances.

Although Taiwanese Hokkien, a regional dialect of Chinese, is widely spoken, Mandarin Chinese is the island nation's official language. Additionally, many people speak English, especially in urban regions.

The traditional arts and crafts of Taiwan include needlework, calligraphy, and pottery. Fine textiles and ceramics have been created by Taiwanese artists for generations, and they are still in high demand today.

Mandopop, sometimes referred to as Taiwanese pop music, has grown in popularity recently. Taiwanese Mandopop artists like Jay Chou and Jolin Tsai have achieved international success and contributed to the internationalization of Taiwanese music.

Baseball and basketball are the two most popular sports in Taiwan, and sports are very significant to the culture there. These sports have produced numerous successful athletes from Taiwan, and the nation frequently organizes international competitions.

Since Taiwan was transferred to Chinese control in 1945, its political status has been a sensitive matter. Following its defeat by the Chinese Communist Party (CCP) in the Chinese Civil War in 1949, the ROC government under Chiang Kai-shek withdrew to Taiwan. Since then, the CCP has declared Taiwan to be a province of China and has promised to use force if necessary to unite Taiwan with the mainland.

The ROC administration, on the other hand, asserts that Taiwan is a sovereign state and that it is the only legal government for all of China, including Taiwan. However, there is disagreement among nations in the international community over this subject, with some acknowledging Taiwan as an independent nation and others viewing it as a part of China.

The connection between Taiwan and the United States has also influenced the country's political landscape. Prior to 1979, when it transferred its diplomatic recognition to the People's Republic of China (PRC), the US recognized the ROC as the legitimate government of China. The US, however, continues to have unofficial relations with Taiwan and is devoted to upholding Taiwan's security.

Despite its political difficulties, Taiwan has recently developed into a thriving democracy. Several successful democratic elections have been held on the island since 1996, when it held its first direct presidential election. A thriving civil society, a free press, and a steadfast dedication to human rights define Taiwan's democratic system.

Taiwan has a distinct and varied history and culture. The island's strategic position at the crossroads of East Asia has made it possible for it to absorb cultural influences from numerous nations and forge its own unique culture. The political situation in Taiwan is complicated because of its interactions with China and the United States. Despite these obstacles, Taiwan has developed into a thriving democracy and economic powerhouse with a rich cultural history that continues to fascinate and inspire people all over the world.

Weather and Climate

East Asian island nation Taiwan, also referred to as the Republic of China, is situated there. It is bordered by the South China Sea to the south, the Taiwan Strait to the west, the East China Sea to the north, and the Philippine Sea to the east. The breathtaking natural beauty, vibrant culture, and delectable food of Taiwan are well-known. It is an intriguing and distinctive area to visit or reside because it is also home to a variety of weather and climate patterns. This guide will examine the many climatic and weather conditions that can be found in Taiwan.

The terrain of Taiwan, which spans an area of about 36,000 square kilometers, is varied and rugged. The eastern and western areas of the island make up its two primary divisions, and they are separated from one another by a mountain range that extends from north to south. Rugged mountain ranges dominate Taiwan's eastern region, whereas lowlands and plains predominate in its western part. Based on altitude and topography, Taiwan's climate is split into four separate zones. The lowlands, hills, high mountains, and offshore islands are examples of these zones.

Lowlands:

The majority of the people live in Taiwan's lowlands, which are on the western half of the island. Temperatures in this area range from 20 to 30 degrees Celsius, and the climate is tropical and humid. In the lowlands, temperatures frequently approach 35 degrees Celsius, and humidity levels can be fairly high, especially in the summer. The lowlands also get a lot of rain, especially from June to October when typhoons are most common.

Hills:

Taiwan's hills are made up of rolling hills and terraced farms, and they are situated in between the lowlands and the high mountains. This area has a temperate climate, which is cooler than that of the lowlands. The hills typically have temperatures between 15 and 25 degrees Celsius, with lower temperatures in the winter. Due to their proximity to the mountains, the hills enjoy more moisture than the lowlands despite receiving less rain than the latter.

High Mountains:

The central and eastern regions of Taiwan are home to the island's high mountains, which are distinguished by their rocky peaks and narrow valleys. This area has a subtropical climate, which is colder than the lowlands and hills. During the winter, temperatures in the upper mountains can fall below freezing, and snowfall is not unusual. Taiwan's high mountains get the majority of the country's precipitation; in some places, this amount can reach 6,000 mm annually.

Offshore Islands:

The offshore islands of Taiwan include Penghu, Kinmen, and Matsu. These islands experience a tropical, humid climate comparable to that of the lowlands. However, because of their proximity to the water, these islands are also vulnerable to typhoons, which can cause major damage.

Typhoons:

In Taiwan, typhoons are common weather occurrences that mainly take place in the summer and early fall. Tropical cyclones called typhoons can produce torrential downpours, ferocious gusts, and flooding as they develop over the Pacific Ocean. Due to its location in the western Pacific Ocean, Taiwan is particularly susceptible to typhoons. In Taiwan, the typhoon season lasts from June to October, with August and September seeing the most activity. Schools and businesses frequently close during this time, and transportation may be hampered by flooding and landslides.

Winter Weather:

Temperatures in Taiwan during the winter often range from 10 to 20 degrees Celsius. However, during this period, snowfall and subfreezing temperatures are possible in the high mountains. In Taiwan, the winter is also the driest season because it receives the least amount of precipitation. This makes it a well-liked time of year for travelers visiting Taiwan, particularly for those who enjoy lower temperatures and outdoor activities like trekking.

Spring Weather:

Taiwan's springtime is characterized by moderate temperatures and sporadic rains. It is a popular season for tourists to visit because this is when cherry blossoms and other flowers begin to bloom. In the spring, the temperature ranges from 15 to 25 degrees Celsius, and the amount of rainfall is usually mild.

Summer Weather:

Taiwan experiences hot, muggy summers with temperatures between 25 and 35 degrees Celsius. In order to escape the heat, people frequently go to air-conditioned establishments or go swimming in the ocean. The humidity can make the temperature feel much hotter. Typhoons are most likely to strike during the summer, so it's crucial to monitor the weather and heed any instructions to evacuate if required.

Fall Weather:

Taiwan's fall weather is similar to that of spring, with warm temperatures and sporadic showers. Due to the pleasant weather and abundance of festivals and events to attend, this is another period when tourists travel to Taiwan. Fall temperatures range from 15 to 25 degrees Celsius, and moderate amounts of rain are normal.

Typhoons, setting, and altitude are a few of the many variables that can influence Taiwan's weather and climate.

The high mountains are subtropical, the high mountains are temperate, the hills are hot and muggy, and the offshore islands are prone to typhoons. In Taiwan, typhoons are a common weather occurrence that can be very destructive, especially in the summer and early fall. However, Taiwan also experiences pleasant weather in the spring, fall, and winter, making it a well-liked vacation spot all year round. Visitors and locals can benefit from knowing Taiwan's weather patterns and being ready for any weather-related events by taking advantage of everything that this stunning nation has to offer.

Festival and Events

Taiwan is a country rich in culture and traditions that are celebrated throughout the year through a variety of festivals and events. From religious ceremonies to food festivals, there is always something happening in Taiwan that can be enjoyed by locals and visitors alike. I will explore some of the most popular festivals and events that take place in Taiwan.

Lunar New Year Festival (春節)

The Lunar New Year Festival, also known as Spring Festival, is one of the most important events in Taiwan. It is celebrated in late January or early February and marks the beginning of the Chinese lunar calendar. The festival lasts for 15 days and is a time for families to come together, exchange gifts, and enjoy traditional foods such as dumplings and rice cakes. Red is a prominent color during the festival, as it is believed to bring good luck and fortune.

One of the highlights of the Lunar New Year Festival in Taiwan is the Taipei Lantern Festival (台北元宵節), which takes place on the 15th day of the festival. The festival features a wide variety of lanterns, including traditional ones made from paper and silk as well as modern LED ones. Visitors can enjoy a range of cultural performances, traditional games, and food stalls.

Lantern Festival (中元節)

The Lantern Festival is another important event in Taiwan, celebrated on the 15th day of the seventh lunar month. It is believed that on this day, the gates of hell are opened, and the spirits of the dead are free to roam the earth. To help guide these spirits back to the afterlife, people light lanterns and release them into the sky or on water.

One of the most popular Lantern Festivals in Taiwan is the Pingxi Sky Lantern Festival (平溪天燈節), which takes place in Pingxi, a small town in New Taipei City. The festival features thousands of lanterns, which are released into the sky by locals and visitors alike. The event also includes cultural performances, food stalls, and traditional games.

Dragon Boat Festival (端午節)

The Dragon Boat Festival, also known as the Duanwu Festival, is celebrated on the fifth day of the fifth lunar month. It commemorates the death of the Chinese poet and minister Qu Yuan, who drowned himself in the Miluo River as a form of protest against government corruption.

Legend has it that local fishermen raced their boats to try and save Qu Yuan, but were too late.

Today, the Dragon Boat Festival is celebrated with dragon boat races, in which teams of paddlers race their boats to the beat of a drum. The festival also features traditional foods such as zongzi, which are sticky rice dumplings wrapped in bamboo leaves.

Mid-Autumn Festival (中秋節)

The Mid-Autumn Festival, also known as the Moon Festival, is celebrated on the 15th day of the eighth lunar month. It is a time for families to come together and enjoy mooncakes, which are traditional pastries filled with sweet or savory fillings.

One of the most popular events during the Mid-Autumn Festival in Taiwan is the Taipei Moon Festival (台北月亮節), which takes place in the Taipei 101 building. The festival features a range of activities, including mooncake making workshops, cultural performances, and traditional games.

Double Ninth Festival (重陽節)

The Double Ninth Festival, also known as the Chongyang Festival, is celebrated on the ninth day of the ninth lunar month. It is a time for people to pay their respects to their elders and enjoy outdoor activities such as hiking and kite flying.

One of the most popular events during the Double Ninth Festival in Taiwan is the Yangmingshan International Kite Festival (陽明山國際風箏節), which takes place in Yangmingshan National Park. The festival features kite flying competitions, cultural performances, and food stalls.

Ghost Month (鬼月)

Ghost Month is a traditional festival in Taiwan that takes place during the seventh lunar month. It is believed that during this month, the gates of hell are opened, and the spirits of the dead are free to roam the earth. To appease these spirits, people offer food, incense, and other offerings at temples and shrines.

One of the most popular events during Ghost Month in Taiwan is the Ghost Festival (中元普渡), which takes place on the 15th day of the month. The festival features street processions, traditional performances, and food stalls.

Taiwan Lantern Festival (台灣燈會)

The Taiwan Lantern Festival is an annual event that takes place in a different city in Taiwan each year. The festival features a wide variety of lanterns, including traditional ones made from paper and silk as well as modern LED ones. Visitors can enjoy a range of cultural performances, traditional games, and food stalls.

One of the most popular Taiwan Lantern Festivals in recent years was the 2020 event in Taichung City, which featured over 30,000 lanterns and attracted millions of visitors.

Taipei International Flora Expo (臺北國際花卉博覽會)

The Taipei International Flora Expo is a biennial event that takes place in Taipei City. The event features a range of exhibitions and displays, showcasing the latest trends in horticulture and floral design. Visitors can enjoy a range of cultural performances, outdoor activities, and food stalls.

The most recent Taipei International Flora Expo was held in 2018 and featured a range of themed pavilions and outdoor installations. The event attracted over 8 million visitors from around the world.

Taiwan Culinary Exhibition (台灣美食展)

The Taiwan Culinary Exhibition is an annual event that takes place in Taipei City. The event features a range of food and beverage exhibitors, showcasing the latest trends in Taiwanese cuisine. Visitors can enjoy a range of food samples, cooking demonstrations, and culinary competitions.

The most recent Taiwan Culinary Exhibition was held in 2021 and featured over 300 exhibitors from Taiwan and around the world. The event attracted over 300,000 visitors, making it one of the largest culinary events in Asia.

Yilan International Children's Folklore and Folkgame Festival (宜蘭國際兒童民俗遊戲節)

The Yilan International Children's Folklore and Folkgame Festival is an annual event that takes place in Yilan County. The festival features a range of traditional games and activities for children, as well as cultural performances and food stalls.

The most recent Yilan International Children's Folklore and Folkgame Festival was held in 2019 and featured over 100,000 participants from Taiwan and around the world. The event is a great way for children to learn about Taiwanese culture and traditions while having fun.

Taiwan is a country rich in culture and traditions that are celebrated throughout the year through a variety of festivals and events. From religious ceremonies to food festivals, there is always something happening in Taiwan that can be enjoyed by locals and visitors alike. Whether you're interested in lanterns, food, or outdoor activities, Taiwan has something for everyone. So, come and experience the unique and colorful festivals and events that Taiwan has to offer.

Best Time to Visit

Taiwan offers much to offer everyone, regardless of your interests in history, gastronomy, shopping, or adventure. Nevertheless, since Taiwan sees a wide diversity of temperatures and weather patterns throughout the year, deciding when to travel there might be challenging. We'll talk about the ideal seasons to visit Taiwan and some of the thrilling experiences you can expect there.

(March – May) spring

Taiwan is in full bloom during the spring, making it one of the greatest times to travel there. It's the perfect time of year for outdoor activities like hiking, cycling, and visiting the countryside because temperatures are often between 15°C and 25°C. The annual Cherry Blossom Festival, which takes place in Taiwan from late February to early April, is the most well-liked occasion of the spring season. Thousands of cherry blossom trees on the island turn gorgeous colours of pink and white at this season, producing a breathtaking visual display.

One of my favorite recollections of my springtime vacation to Taiwan is the day trip I did to Yangmingshan National Park. The park, which is nearby Taipei, is well-known for its hot springs, hiking paths, and stunning mountain views. The cherry blossoms are in full bloom in the spring, which is a particularly lovely time to visit the park. I hiked throughout the park all day, admiring the stunning views. I relaxed in a natural hot spring in the evening while admiring the mountains' setting.

Summer (June - August)

Temperatures in Taiwan's summer range from 25°C to 35°C, making it hot and muggy. Even though it's hot, summer is still a popular time to travel to Taiwan because it's the busiest travel period and there are many of outdoor activities and festivals to take part in. In the summer, a large number of people and visitors frequent Taiwan's beaches and coastal communities to cool off in the water.

When I went surfing in Kenting on my summer trip to Taiwan, it remains one of my greatest memories. The southern Taiwanese seaside town of Kenting is renowned for its stunning beaches and top-notch surf. I stayed in Kenting for a week, surfing during the day and checking out the town's eateries and night markets at night. Live music, spontaneous street performances, and large throngs of people taking advantage of the balmy summer evenings created an electrifying scene in Kenting during the summer.

Fall (September through November)

With the mountains and woods of Taiwan changing to vivid hues of red, orange, and yellow throughout the autumn, it's possible that this is the country's most gorgeous season. Autumn in Taiwan is a great time to visit the countryside and national parks because the temperatures are warm, ranging from 20 to 30 degrees. One of the most important celebrations in Taiwan is the Mid-Autumn Festival, which takes place on the fifteenth day of the eighth lunar month (often in September or October). Families and friends congregate to celebrate by eating mooncakes, lighting lanterns, and gazing at the full moon.

One of my favorite recollections of my autumn vacation to Taiwan is the bicycle tour I had through the East Coast Scenic Area. A 170-kilometer stretch of coastline known for its craggy cliffs, azure waters, and spectacular views is known as the East Coast Scenic Area. I cycled the coast for five days while staying in small towns and villages. Cycling through the Taroko Gorge, a breathtaking marble canyon that is one of Taiwan's most well-known natural features, was the excursion's high point.

(December to February) Winter

Taiwan experiences a warm winter with average highs of 15°C in the south and 10°C to 20°C in the north. Even though the winter is Taiwan's off-season for tourists, it's still a fantastic time to go if you want a more laid-back and tranquil vacation. Winter is a particularly popular time to visit Taiwan's hot springs since so many locals and visitors seek refuge in the warm waters from the bitter cold.

One of my fondest memories from my winter trip to Taiwan is visiting Beitou's hot springs. Beitou, a Taipei suburb, is well-known for its hot springs and bathhouses designed in the Japanese style. I spent the day lazing around in the traditional bathhouses and soaking in the hot springs, which were surrounded by lovely gardens and gorgeous vistas. I had a great hot pot dinner in the evening at a nearby restaurant, which was the ideal way to warm up after a day outdoors in the chilly weather.

What therefore makes Taiwan the ideal destination? It all depends on your hobbies and the activities you wish to perform while you're away. The best time to visit if you want to see the cherry blossoms is in the spring. Summer is the ideal time to visit Taiwan's coastal communities and beaches if you love the beach. Autumn is the best season for nature lovers to see Taiwan's national parks and countryside. Winter is a perfect season to visit Taiwan's hot springs and traditional bathhouses if you're seeking for a quiet and relaxed vacation.

No matter what season you travel, Taiwan is a beautiful location that has something to offer everyone. Taiwan offers everything, regardless of your interests in history, culture, cuisine, or adventure. Pack your bags and get ready to discover Taiwan's charm and beauty for yourself.

Visa and Travel Documents

To enter Taiwan, most foreign nationals need to obtain a visa or a travel authorization document, depending on their nationality and the length and purpose of their stay.

In this guide, I will explore the different types of visas and travel documents available for Taiwan and provide you with all the necessary information to plan your trip to this beautiful country.

Types of Visas and Travel Documents for Taiwan:

Visa-Exempt Entry:
Citizens of certain countries are eligible for visa-exempt entry to Taiwan, which allows them to stay in the country for a maximum of 90 days without a visa. To enter Taiwan under visa-exempt status, travelers must have a passport with at least six months of validity and a confirmed return or onward ticket.

The following countries are currently eligible for visa-exempt entry to Taiwan:

Australia

Austria

Belgium

Canada

Czech Republic

Denmark

Estonia

Finland

France

Germany

Greece

Hungary

Iceland

Ireland

Israel

Italy

Japan

South Korea

Latvia

Liechtenstein

Lithuania

Luxembourg

Malta

Monaco

the Netherlands

New Zealand

Norway

Poland

Portugal

Slovakia

Slovenia

Spain

Sweden

Switzerland

the United Kingdom

the United States

Landing Visa:

Citizens of certain countries who are not eligible for visa-exempt entry to Taiwan may still be able to obtain a visa upon arrival at the airport. This type of visa is called a landing visa or visa on arrival and is valid for a maximum of 30 days. Travelers who wish to obtain a landing visa must have a passport with at least six months of validity, a confirmed return or onward ticket, and proof of sufficient funds for their stay in Taiwan.

The following countries are currently eligible for a landing visa to Taiwan:

Cambodia

India

Indonesia

Laos

Malaysia

Myanmar

the Philippines

Singapore

Thailand

Vietnam

Visitor Visa:

Citizens of countries that is not eligible for visa-exempt entry or a landing visa must obtain a visitor visa from a Taiwan representative office or embassy in their home country before traveling to Taiwan. The visitor visa is issued for a maximum of 60 days and can be extended for up to 120 days.

To apply for a visitor visa, travelers must provide a passport with at least six months of validity, a completed visa application form, a recent passport-sized photograph, and proof of sufficient funds for their stay in Taiwan. Depending on the purpose of the visit, travelers may also need to provide additional documents, such as a letter of invitation from a Taiwan-based organization or a letter from their employer.

Resident Visa:
Foreign nationals who wish to live and work in Taiwan for an extended period must obtain a resident visa. The resident visa is issued for a period of up to three years and can be renewed upon expiration.

To apply for a resident visa, applicants must provide a passport with at least six months of validity, a completed visa application form, a recent passport-sized photograph, and proof of sufficient funds for their stay in Taiwan. Depending on the purpose of the visit, applicants may also need to provide additional documents, such as a work permit or proof of enrollment in a Taiwan-based educational institution.

eVisa:
Taiwan also offers an eVisa program for citizens of certain countries who wish to visit Taiwan for tourism, business, or medical purposes. The eVisa is valid for a maximum of 90 days and allows multiple entries to Taiwan during its validity.

To apply for an eVisa, travelers must provide a passport with at least six months of validity, a recent passport-sized photograph, and proof of sufficient funds for their stay in

Taiwan. The application can be submitted online, and the processing time is usually three business days.

The following countries are currently eligible for the eVisa program:

Bhutan
India
Indonesia
The Philippines
Russia
Thailand
Vietnam

Travel Authorization Certificate (TAC):

The Travel Authorization Certificate (TAC) is a new electronic travel authorization document that allows citizens of certain countries to visit Taiwan for tourism or business purposes for up to 90 days without a visa. The TAC is valid for two years from the date of issue and allows multiple entries to Taiwan during its validity.

To apply for a TAC, travelers must provide a passport with at least six months of validity, a recent passport-sized photograph, and proof of sufficient funds for their stay in Taiwan. The application can be submitted online, and the processing time is usually three business days.

The following countries are currently eligible for the TAC:

Cambodia
India
Indonesia
Laos
Myanmar
The Philippines
Vietnam

Taiwan offers a range of visas and travel documents to foreign nationals depending on their nationality, purpose of visit, and length of stay. Whether you are traveling to Taiwan for tourism, business, or to live and work, there is a visa or travel authorization document that will suit your needs.

Before planning your trip to Taiwan, it is essential to check the latest visa and travel requirements to ensure that you have all the necessary documents and can enter the country smoothly.

Transportation

Taiwan despite its small size, it boasts a highly efficient and modern transportation system that connects its major cities and towns. In this guide, I will explore the various modes of transportation available in Taiwan, from high-speed rail to local buses, and examine how they contribute to the island's economy, environment, and way of life.

High-Speed Rail

The Taiwan High-Speed Rail (THSR) system is one of the most impressive transportation networks in the world. Built at a cost of US$15 billion, it covers a distance of 345 kilometers (214 miles) and connects the cities of Taipei, Taoyuan, Hsinchu, Taichung, Chiayi, Tainan, and Kaohsiung. The trains travel at speeds of up to 300 kilometers per hour (186 miles per hour) and offer passengers a comfortable, reliable, and fast way to travel between Taiwan's major cities.

The THSR system has had a significant impact on Taiwan's economy since it was launched in 2007. It has reduced travel times between cities, making it easier for people to do business and attend meetings. It has also encouraged tourism by making it easier for visitors to explore Taiwan's many attractions. The THSR system has also created jobs and generated revenue for local businesses, including hotels, restaurants, and shops.

Public Buses

Taiwan's public bus system is also highly efficient and reliable. Buses are operated by both public and private companies and cover both short and long distances. The buses are clean, air-conditioned, and equipped with modern amenities such as Wi-Fi and USB charging ports.

One of the advantages of Taiwan's public bus system is its affordability. Fares are relatively cheap, and passengers can pay using cash or rechargeable IC cards. The buses also offer a high level of convenience, as they run frequently and cover a wide network of routes. This makes it easy for people to travel to work, school, or leisure activities.

Another advantage of Taiwan's public bus system is its focus on sustainability. Many of the buses run on natural gas or electricity, reducing their impact on the environment. In addition, the government has implemented policies to encourage people to use public transportation, such as providing tax incentives for companies that offer employee bus passes.

Metro Systems

Taiwan's two largest cities, Taipei and Kaohsiung, have metro systems that serve millions of passengers every day. The Taipei Metro, also known as the MRT, has six lines and covers a distance of 131 kilometers (81 miles). The Kaohsiung Metro has two lines and covers a distance of 46 kilometers (29 miles). Both systems are clean, safe, and efficient, and offer passengers a fast and convenient way to travel within the cities.

One of the advantages of Taiwan's metro systems is their integration with other modes of transportation. Passengers can easily transfer from the metro to buses, trains, or high-speed rail, making it easy to travel across the island. The metro systems also offer a high level of accessibility, with elevators, escalators, and ramps for passengers with disabilities.

Another advantage of Taiwan's metro systems is their focus on sustainability. Both systems run on electricity, reducing their impact on the environment. The government has also implemented policies to encourage people to use the metro, such as offering discounts for passengers who use rechargeable IC cards.

Bicycles

Bicycles are a popular mode of transportation in Taiwan, especially in urban areas. Many people use bicycles to travel short distances, such as to work or school. Bicycles are also a popular way to explore Taiwan's many scenic routes and attractions, such as the Sun Moon Lake and the Taroko Gorge.

To encourage people to use bicycles, the Taiwanese government has implemented a number of initiatives. For example, it has built dedicated bike lanes in many urban areas, making it safer for cyclists to travel. It has also implemented a bike-sharing program in cities such as Taipei and Kaohsiung, allowing people to rent bicycles for a low fee. In addition, the government has provided tax incentives for companies that offer bike-sharing programs for their employees.

One of the benefits of using bicycles is their low impact on the environment. Bicycles do not emit any greenhouse gases, making them an environmentally friendly mode of transportation. In addition, cycling is a form of exercise, which has health benefits for the individual rider.

Taxis

Taxis are also a popular mode of transportation in Taiwan, especially for people who want to travel quickly or do not have access to a car. Taxis are relatively cheap compared to other countries, and passengers can choose between metered taxis or fixed-price taxis. In addition, many taxis are equipped with GPS systems, making it easier for passengers to navigate to their destination.

However, one of the downsides of using taxis in Taiwan is the heavy traffic in urban areas. Traffic congestion can make it difficult for taxis to travel quickly, and passengers may end up paying more for longer travel times. In addition, some taxi drivers may not speak English, which can make it difficult for foreign visitors to communicate with them.

Air Travel

Taiwan has two major airports, Taoyuan International Airport and Kaohsiung International Airport, which serve as hubs for international and domestic flights. Taoyuan International Airport is one of the busiest airports in Asia, serving more than 40 million passengers per year.

Air travel is a convenient way to travel long distances in Taiwan or to other countries. Taiwan has direct flights to many destinations around the world, including the United States, Europe, and Asia. In addition, air travel is relatively fast compared to other modes of transportation, allowing passengers to save time on their travels.

However, one of the downsides of air travel is its impact on the environment. Airplanes emit greenhouse gasses and contribute to air pollution, making it a less environmentally friendly mode of transportation. In addition, air travel can be expensive compared to other modes of transportation, making it less accessible to some people.

Taiwan's transportation system is a vital component of its economy, environment, and way of life. The various modes of transportation available, from high-speed rail to bicycles, offer passengers a range of options for their travels. The government's focus on sustainability and accessibility has made Taiwan a model for other countries to follow. Whether for business or leisure, travelers to Taiwan can expect a reliable, efficient, and modern transportation system to take them where they need to go.

Accommodation

Taiwan is a beautiful island nation known for its vibrant culture, rich history, and stunning natural beauty. As a popular tourist destination, Taiwan offers a wide range of accommodation options that cater to all types of travelers.

From luxury hotels to budget-friendly hostels, Taiwan has it all. One of the most popular types of accommodation in Taiwan is the traditional Taiwanese guesthouse, also known as a "minsu". These charming guest houses offer a unique and authentic Taiwanese experience, with comfortable rooms decorated in traditional Taiwanese style and home-cooked meals made with fresh, local ingredients.

As a tourist visiting Taiwan, I had the pleasure of staying in a traditional Taiwanese guesthouse during my trip. My journey began with a search for the perfect accommodation that would allow me to fully immerse myself in the local culture and way of life.

After hours of research, I stumbled upon a beautiful guesthouse located in the heart of Taiwan's scenic countryside. I was immediately drawn to its rustic charm and quaint atmosphere, and I knew that this was the perfect place for me to stay during my visit.

Upon arrival, I was warmly welcomed by the guesthouse owners, a lovely couple who had lived in the area their entire lives. They showed me to my room, which was decorated with beautiful hand-painted murals and traditional Taiwanese furnishings. The room was cozy and comfortable, with all the amenities I needed for a relaxing stay.

Each morning, I was treated to a delicious breakfast made with fresh, locally-sourced ingredients. I enjoyed chatting with the owners over breakfast and learning more about the local area and its history.

One of the highlights of my stay was a guided tour of the surrounding countryside, led by the guesthouse owners. They took me on a hike through the lush green forests and showed me hidden waterfalls and other natural wonders that I never would have found on my own.

Overall, my stay in the traditional Taiwanese guesthouse was a truly memorable experience. The warm hospitality and authentic local culture made me feel right at home, and I left Taiwan with a deeper appreciation for this beautiful island nation and its people.

Taiwan is a beautiful and vibrant country that attracts millions of visitors each year. While guesthouses are a popular form of accommodation for budget-conscious travelers, there are many other options available that offer comfort, luxury, and unique experiences.

Hotels are a great option for those who want the convenience and amenities of a traditional accommodation. There are many hotels in Taiwan that cater to all kinds of travelers, from budget-friendly options to luxury resorts. Some popular hotel chains in Taiwan include Grand Hyatt, Shangri-La, and Mandarin Oriental. These hotels offer a range of services, such as restaurants, spas, and fitness centers, to make your stay as comfortable and enjoyable as possible.

Another popular form of accommodation in Taiwan is the homestay. Homestays provide a unique opportunity to experience local culture and customs by staying with a local family. In addition to providing a comfortable place to stay, many homestays offer home-cooked meals, language lessons, and cultural activities. Homestays are particularly popular in rural areas, where visitors can experience the traditional way of life and connect with the local community.

For those who prefer a more unique and unconventional experience, camping is a popular option in Taiwan. Camping combines the comfort of a hotel with the natural beauty of the outdoors. There are many camping sites in Taiwan that offer luxurious tents or cabins in beautiful locations, such as the mountains or the beach. Some camping sites even offer hot springs or spa services for added relaxation.

Lastly, for those who want to immerse themselves in nature, camping is a great option in Taiwan. There are many campsites located in national parks and scenic areas throughout Taiwan. Camping allows you to enjoy the beautiful scenery and natural environment, while also providing a sense of adventure and freedom.

Taiwan offers a variety of accommodation options to suit all kinds of travelers. From traditional hotels to unique experiences like homestays, camping, and camping, there is something for everyone. No matter what type of accommodation you choose, you are sure to have a memorable and enjoyable stay in Taiwan.

Traditional Taiwanese Cuisine

Taiwanese cuisine is an amalgamation of various cultural influences from China, Japan, Southeast Asia, and indigenous Taiwanese cuisine. With its rich history and diverse culinary traditions, Taiwan has developed a unique cuisine that is known for its bold flavors, colorful presentations, and use of fresh ingredients. In this guide, I will explore traditional Taiwanese cuisine and the cultural influences that have shaped it over time.

Taiwan's culinary traditions date back thousands of years, with indigenous tribes being the earliest inhabitants of the island. The aboriginal tribes of Taiwan relied heavily on hunting, fishing, and farming for their food, and their diet consisted of wild game, fish, millet, and taro. Over time, Chinese immigrants began settling in Taiwan, bringing with them their own culinary traditions.

During the Qing dynasty (1644-1911), Taiwan became a province of China, and as a result, Chinese cuisine became more prevalent on the island. Later, during the Japanese colonial period (1895-1945), Japanese culinary influences also had a significant impact on Taiwanese cuisine. After World War II, Taiwan became a separate entity, and the government launched a campaign to promote Taiwanese cuisine, resulting in the emergence of many traditional Taiwanese dishes.

Taiwanese cuisine is characterized by the use of fresh and locally sourced ingredients, such as seafood, vegetables, fruits, and herbs. Taiwan's tropical climate allows for a wide variety of fruits and vegetables to grow year-round, including pineapple, mango, guava, papaya, and taro. Taiwanese cuisine is also known for its bold and complex flavors, which are achieved through the use of spices, sauces, and seasonings.

Some of the most popular spices and seasonings used in Taiwanese cuisine include ginger, garlic, scallions, sesame oil, soy sauce, rice wine, and chili peppers. These ingredients are used to flavor dishes such as braised pork belly (lu rou fan), stir-fried noodles (chow mein), and steamed buns (baozi).

In addition to the use of fresh ingredients and bold flavors, Taiwanese cuisine is also known for its colorful presentations. Traditional Taiwanese dishes are often served in a variety of small plates, with each dish highlighting a different flavor and texture.

Popular Taiwanese Dishes

Beef Noodle Soup

Beef noodle soup is one of Taiwan's most famous dishes, and it is widely regarded as the country's national dish. This hearty soup is made with tender chunks of beef, wheat noodles, and a flavorful broth that is seasoned with soy sauce, ginger, and star anise. It is often served with a variety of toppings, including green onions, cilantro, and pickled vegetables.

Bubble Tea

Bubble tea, also known as pearl milk tea, originated in Taiwan in the 1980s and has since become a popular drink around the world. This sweet and creamy tea is made with black tea, milk, and sugar, and it is served with chewy tapioca pearls.

Fried Chicken

Fried chicken is a popular street food in Taiwan, and it is often served with a variety of dipping sauces, such as sweet chili sauce and soy sauce. The chicken is coated in a mixture of flour, cornstarch, and spices before being deep-fried to crispy perfection.

Braised Pork Belly

Braised pork belly is a classic Taiwanese dish that consists of tender chunks of pork belly that have been slow-cooked in a soy sauce-based broth. It is often served over a bed of steamed rice and topped with pickled vegetables and a fried egg.

Oyster Omelette

Oyster omelette is a popular street food in Taiwan that consists of a fluffy omelette filled with fresh oysters, vegetables, and a sweet and savory sauce. The omelette is pan-fried until crispy on the outside and tender on the inside.

Stinky Tofu

Stinky tofu is a polarizing dish in Taiwanese cuisine that is known for its pungent aroma and strong flavor. The tofu is fermented in a mixture of milk, vegetables, and spices, giving it a distinct smell and flavor. It is often deep-fried and served with pickled vegetables and chili sauce.

Scallion Pancakes

Scallion pancakes are a popular breakfast food in Taiwan that is made with dough of flour, water, and scallions. The dough is rolled out, fried until crispy, and served with a sweet and savory dipping sauce.

Taiwanese cuisine has been influenced by various cultural traditions over the years, including Chinese, Japanese, and Southeast Asian cuisine. These influences have contributed to the unique flavor profile and cooking techniques found in traditional Taiwanese cuisine.

Chinese cuisine has had the most significant impact on Taiwanese cuisine, with many traditional Taiwanese dishes having roots in Chinese cooking. Some of the most common Chinese dishes found in Taiwan include dumplings, hot pot, and stir-fried noodles.

One of the most popular dishes in Taiwanese cuisine that has Chinese roots is beef noodle soup. This dish originated in China's Sichuan province and was brought to Taiwan by Chinese immigrants. Taiwanese chefs added their own twist to the dish, using local ingredients such as beef and wheat noodles and adding their own blend of spices to the broth.

During the Japanese colonial period, Japanese cuisine had a significant impact on Taiwanese cuisine. Many Japanese dishes, such as tempura and sushi, were introduced to Taiwan during this time. However, the most significant influence on Taiwanese cuisine was the Japanese bento box.

The bento box is a traditional Japanese lunch box that consists of rice, vegetables, and meat or fish. Taiwanese chefs adapted the bento box, using local ingredients and adding their own twist to the traditional Japanese dish. Today, the Taiwanese bento box is a popular lunchtime meal that is served at street vendors and restaurants throughout the country.

Taiwan's proximity to Southeast Asia has also had a significant influence on the country's cuisine. Many Southeast Asian dishes, such as curry and laksa, have become popular in Taiwan in recent years. Taiwanese chefs have adapted these dishes, using local ingredients and adding their own unique twist to the recipes.

One of the most popular Southeast Asian dishes in Taiwan

is Thai-style hot pot. This dish consists of a spicy broth made with lemongrass, chili, and lime, which is used to cook a variety of meats and vegetables. Taiwanese chefs have added their own twist to the dish, using local ingredients such as seafood and tofu and adding their own blend of spices to the broth.

Taiwanese cuisine is a unique blend of cultural influences from China, Japan, Southeast Asia, and indigenous Taiwanese cuisine. With its bold flavors, colorful presentations, and use of fresh ingredients, Taiwanese cuisine has become one of the most popular cuisines in the world.

From beef noodle soup to bubble tea, Taiwanese cuisine has something to offer for every palate. As Taiwan continues to grow and evolve, its culinary traditions will continue to reflect the country's rich history and diverse cultural influences.

One of my most memorable experiences with traditional Taiwanese cuisine was during a visit to Taipei, where I had the opportunity to try some of the local delicacies. One of the standout dishes that I tried was the famous Taiwanese beef noodle soup. The broth was rich and flavorful, made from simmering beef bones and aromatic herbs for hours on end. The tender slices of beef and chewy noodles added texture and depth to the soup, and I could taste the care and attention that went into crafting such a delicious dish.

Another standout dish was the oyster omelet, a popular street food that is a must-try for anyone visiting Taiwan. The omelet was cooked to perfection, with a crispy exterior and a fluffy, flavorful interior. The plump, juicy oysters added a burst of umami flavor that balanced out the dish perfectly.

One dish that really surprised me was stinky tofu. Despite its reputation for being an acquired taste, I found it to be surprisingly delicious. The pungent aroma of the fermented tofu gave way to a complex, savory flavor that was unlike anything I had ever tasted before. Paired with a spicy dipping sauce, it was the perfect snack to enjoy while exploring the bustling night markets of Taipei.

One of my favorite meals during my visit to Taiwan was at a small, family-run restaurant in Tainan, where I was served a variety of traditional Taiwanese dishes. The standout dish was the braised pork belly, which was cooked to perfection and melted in my mouth. The flavors were rich and complex, with hints of soy sauce, ginger, and star anise. It was served with steamed rice and a variety of vegetable dishes, each one bursting with flavor and freshness.

Overall, my experiences with traditional Taiwanese cuisine were nothing short of incredible. From the bold flavors to the elegant presentation, every dish was crafted with care and attention to detail. I can't wait to visit Taiwan again and explore even more of the country's culinary delights.

Night markets in Taiwan are an integral part of the country's vibrant culture and are renowned for their bustling energy, eclectic food offerings, and unique shopping experiences. These markets are open-air bazaars that operate during the evenings, and they offer a wide range of street food, clothing, and souvenirs. Taiwan has over 100 night markets spread across the island, each with its own distinct character and style.

The origins of night markets in Taiwan can be traced back to the period of Japanese rule, which lasted from 1895 to 1945. During this time, the Japanese established the first night market in Taipei, which was called Shilin Night Market. The market was located near the Shilin railway station and was set up to cater to the needs of Japanese trus stationed in the area. The market initially sold only basic goods such as vegetables, meat, and fish, but it eventually expanded to include clothing, toys, and other items.

After World War II, Taiwan was returned to Chinese rule, and the night market culture continued to thrive. As Taiwan's economy grew, so did the night markets, which became a popular destination for locals and tourists alike. The markets evolved to include a wide variety of food stalls, gaming booths, and entertainment venues. Today, Taiwan's night markets are considered some of the best in the world, attracting visitors from all over the globe.

Taiwan's night markets are known for their lively and energetic atmosphere. Visitors are greeted with the sounds of music, the aroma of food, and the chatter of people haggling over prices. The markets are usually held in open-air spaces, with vendors selling their wares from makeshift stalls and carts.

Food is one of the main attractions of Taiwan's night markets. Taiwanese cuisine is a fusion of Chinese, Japanese, and indigenous influences, and the night markets offer a wide variety of dishes that reflect this diverse culinary heritage. Some of the most popular dishes include stinky tofu, oyster omelets, bubble tea, and fried chicken. Many of these dishes are unique to Taiwan and cannot be found anywhere else in the world.

Night market

Apart from food, Taiwan's night markets also offer a range of shopping opportunities. Visitors can purchase clothing, accessories, souvenirs, and electronic goods. Many vendors specialize in handmade crafts and traditional Taiwanese products, such as lacquerware and bamboo baskets.

The night markets are also a hub for entertainment, with gaming booths, arcades, and street performers adding to the festive atmosphere. Visitors can participate in games such as shooting galleries, balloon darts, and ring toss, and win prizes ranging from stuffed animals to electronic gadgets. Street performers, such as musicians, dancers, and magicians, entertain crowds with their talents and add to the vibrant energy of the markets.

Night markets are an integral part of Taiwanese society and have played a significant role in shaping the country's cultural identity. They serve as a platform for entrepreneurs and small business owners, providing a space for them to showcase their products and services. Many vendors are members of the local community and have been operating their stalls for generations, passing down their skills and knowledge to future generations.

The markets are also a social gathering place for friends and families. Taiwanese people place great importance on the concept of "guanxi," which refers to the building of relationships through social interactions. The night markets offer an opportunity for people to connect with others in their community, bond over food and entertainment, and create lasting memories.

Night markets are also a source of pride for Taiwanese people and serve as a way of showcasing their culture and traditions to visitors from around the world. The markets provide a glimpse into the unique characteristics of Taiwanese society, such as its culinary traditions, entrepreneurial spirit, and friendly, welcoming nature.

Night markets also have an economic significance, as they contribute to the local economy by providing jobs and generating revenue. Many vendors rely on the income generated from their night market stalls as their primary source of livelihood. The markets also attract tourists, who spend money on food, shopping, and entertainment, contributing to the local economy and supporting local businesses.

Despite their popularity and cultural significance, Taiwan's night markets face several challenges that threaten their survival. One of the main challenges is the changing landscape of the retail industry, with more people shopping online and traditional brick-and-mortar stores struggling to stay afloat. This trend has affected night markets as well, with some vendors struggling to attract customers and keep their businesses profitable.

Another challenge is the increasing regulation of night markets by local governments. In recent years, there have been calls to regulate night markets more closely, with some local officials concerned about issues such as food safety, noise pollution, and traffic congestion. While these regulations are necessary to ensure the safety and well-being of visitors, they can also make it more difficult for vendors to operate their businesses and maintain their livelihoods.

Finally, Taiwan's night markets are also facing competition from other destinations in Asia that offer similar experiences, such as night markets in Thailand and South Korea. To remain competitive, Taiwan's night markets need to continue to innovate and evolve, offering new and unique experiences that set them apart from their competitors.

Taiwan's night markets are an integral part of the country's cultural identity, offering a unique blend of food, shopping, and entertainment. They serve as a platform for small business owners and entrepreneurs, providing a space for them to showcase their products and services. The markets also play a significant role in promoting social interactions and strengthening community ties, while contributing to the local economy.

However, Taiwan's night markets also face several challenges that threaten their survival, including changing retail trends, increasing regulation, and competition from other destinations in Asia. To remain relevant and competitive, Taiwan's night markets must continue to innovate and evolve, offering new and unique experiences that cater to the changing needs of visitors and consumers. Overall, Taiwan's night markets are a testament to the country's rich cultural heritage and entrepreneurial spirit, and they remain a must-visit destination for anyone interested in experiencing the vibrancy and energy of Taiwanese society.

Night markets are an essential part of Taiwanese culture, offering a bustling and colorful atmosphere, delicious street food, and a wide variety of products for sale. From traditional snacks and handmade crafts to trendy fashion and electronic gadgets, Taiwan's night markets are a popular destination for both locals and tourists alike.

As a visitor to Taiwan, I was eager to explore the night markets and experience the vibrant energy that they are known for. After some research, I decided to start my adventure at the famous Shilin Night Market in Taipei, the largest and most well-known of all the night markets in Taiwan.

The night market was located in the Shilin District, a bustling area filled with shops, restaurants, and entertainment venues. As I arrived at the market, I was immediately struck by the lively atmosphere and the aroma of delicious food wafting through the air.

Stalls lined the streets, offering everything from grilled meat skewers to bubble tea, fried chicken to stinky tofu, and much more. As I explored the various stalls, I was amazed at the sheer variety of street food available, each vendor offering their own unique twist on traditional Taiwanese dishes.

One of my favorite snacks was the famous "gua bao," a soft steamed bun filled with braised pork, cilantro, and peanut powder. Another must-try was the oyster omelet, a savory dish made with eggs, oysters, and a sweet and tangy sauce.

As I wandered through the night market, I also had the chance to check out a variety of other products for sale, including handmade crafts, clothing, and accessories. One stall that caught my eye was selling intricate paper cutouts, each one delicately crafted with incredible detail and precision.

I also enjoyed browsing the stalls selling unique souvenirs, such as colorful Taiwanese postcards and traditional hand-painted fans. It was clear that each vendor took great pride in their craft, and I appreciated the opportunity to support local businesses and artisans.

As the night wore on, the energy of the market only seemed to grow, with crowds of locals and tourists alike filling the streets. The sounds of street performers, live music, and carnival games added to the festive atmosphere, making it a truly unforgettable experience.

After several hours of exploring the Shilin Night Market, I

reluctantly headed back to my hotel, already looking forward to the next night market adventure. Over the course of my trip, I visited several other night markets in Taiwan, each with their own unique charm and character.

One market that stood out to me was the Fengjia Night Market in Taichung, known for its trendy fashion and electronic gadgets. As a self-proclaimed tech nerd, I was excited to check out the latest gadgets and gizmos on offer.

The market was located in the bustling Fengjia district, and as I approached the entrance, I was immediately struck by the colorful lights and the sounds of electronic dance music. Inside, I found row after row of stalls selling the latest tech gadgets, from smartphone accessories to gaming peripherals.

But it wasn't just electronics on offer - the food was just as impressive, with vendors selling everything from traditional Taiwanese street food to fusion dishes with a modern twist. One dish that caught my eye was the "stinky tofu hot pot," a unique take on the classic hot pot dish featuring the infamous Taiwanese delicacy - stinky tofu.

As I wandered through the market, I also had the

opportunity to check out some of the trendy fashion stalls, selling everything from the latest streetwear to unique vintage pieces. I even managed to find a few items to add to my own wardrobe, including a stylish denim jacket and a pair of colorful sneakers.

But it wasn't just the food and fashion that made the Fengjia Night Market so memorable - it was the people I was struck by the friendly and welcoming atmosphere, with vendors and customers alike chatting and laughing with one another. As I sat down to enjoy my stinky tofu hot pot, I struck up a conversation with a group of local students who were eager to practice their English and share their favorite spots in the city.

Through my conversations with locals, I learned that night markets are not just a place to shop and eat, but also a cultural hub where people come together to socialize and connect. It was a reminder that even as a visitor, I could experience the warmth and hospitality that Taiwan is known for.

One of my most memorable experiences at a night market was at the Raohe Street Night Market in Taipei. As I explored the market, I stumbled upon a traditional

Taiwanese puppet show, with intricate hand-crafted puppets telling the story of a mythical dragon and a brave hero.

The puppeteers were dressed in elaborate costumes and used intricate movements and music to bring the story to life. Despite not speaking the language, I was captivated by the performance and the enthusiasm of the crowd.

After the show, I struck up a conversation with one of the puppeteers, who explained the history and significance of traditional puppetry in Taiwanese culture. It was a fascinating glimpse into a rich cultural tradition that I might have otherwise missed.

As my trip to Taiwan came to a close, I found myself reflecting on the incredible experiences I had at the night markets. While each market was unique, they all shared a common thread - a celebration of local culture and community.

Whether it was through the delicious food, the colorful crafts, or the lively entertainment, the night markets offered a window into the heart of Taiwan. And as a visitor, I felt fortunate to be able to share in that experience, to connect with locals, and to make memories that would last a lifetime.

Night markets in Taiwan are a must-see attraction for anyone visiting the country. From the bustling streets and delicious street food to the friendly people and unique crafts, the night markets offer a truly immersive and unforgettable experience. As a visitor, I feel lucky to have been able to explore these vibrant cultural hubs and to connect with the people and traditions that make Taiwan so special.

Bubble Tea

Bubble Tea, also known as Boba Tea or Pearl Milk Tea, is a Taiwanese drink that has taken the world by storm. It is a beverage made from tea, milk, sugar, and tapioca pearls, which are small, chewy balls made from tapioca starch. Bubble Tea originated in Taiwan in the 1980s and has since become a global phenomenon, with Bubble Tea shops popping up in cities all over the world. In this guide, I will explore the history of Bubble Tea in Taiwan, the cultural significance of this drink, and its impact on the global food and beverage industry.

Bubble Tea originated in Taiwan in the 1980s. According to legend, a tea house owner named Liu Han-Chieh created the drink by adding tapioca balls to his iced tea, thus creating a unique and refreshing beverage. The drink quickly became popular, and other tea houses began to create their own versions of Bubble Tea. By the 1990s, Bubble Tea had become a staple of Taiwanese street food culture, with small shops and street vendors selling the drink to locals and tourists alike.

The first Bubble Tea shops were small, family-run businesses that specialized in making Bubble Tea. These shops were often located in night markets, where they would stay open late into the night, catering to night owls and party-goers. Over time, Bubble Tea shops began to expand, with some shops offering a wider range of drinks and snacks, while others expanded into chains with multiple locations throughout Taiwan.

Today, Bubble Tea is an integral part of Taiwanese culture, and is enjoyed by people of all ages and backgrounds. It is sold everywhere from small street vendors to high-end cafes, and is considered a must-try for anyone visiting Taiwan.

Bubble Tea has become more than just a drink in Taiwan; it is a cultural phenomenon that has come to represent the country's vibrant street food culture. It is a drink that is enjoyed by people of all ages, and has become a symbol of Taiwanese identity.

One reason why Bubble Tea has become so popular in Taiwan is because it is a drink that can be customized to suit individual tastes. Bubble Tea shops offer a wide variety of flavors and toppings, which means that people can create their own unique drinks. This has led to a culture of experimentation, with people constantly trying new combinations of flavors and toppings.

Another reason why Bubble Tea is so popular in Taiwan is because of its social significance. In Taiwan, it is common for people to meet up with friends or colleagues at Bubble Tea shops. It is a social activity that brings people together, and is often used as an excuse to catch up with old friends or make new ones.

In addition, Bubble Tea has become a source of pride for many Taiwanese people. It is a drink that has gained global recognition, and has put Taiwan on the map as a leader in the food and beverage industry. For many Taiwanese people, Bubble Tea is a way to showcase their culture and heritage to the world.

Bubble Tea has had a significant impact on the global food and beverage industry. Since its inception in Taiwan in the 1980s, Bubble Tea has spread throughout the world, becoming a global phenomenon.

One reason for Bubble Tea's global popularity is its unique taste and texture. The combination of tea, milk, sugar, and tapioca pearls creates a drink that is both refreshing and satisfying. It is a drink that appeals to people of all ages and backgrounds, and has become a staple of street food culture in many countries.

Another reason for Bubble Tea's popularity is its versatility. Bubble Tea shops offer a wide variety of flavors and toppings, which means that people can create their own unique drinks. This has led to a culture of experimentation and innovation, with Bubble Tea shops constantly coming up with new flavors and combinations to attract customers.

Bubble Tea has also had a significant impact on the economy, both in Taiwan and in other countries. In Taiwan, the Bubble Tea industry generates billions of dollars in revenue each year, and has created thousands of jobs. In other countries, Bubble Tea shops have become a popular business venture, with entrepreneurs opening up their own shops to cater to the demand for this drink.

However, the global popularity of Bubble Tea has not been without controversy. Some people have raised concerns about the health effects of consuming large amounts of sugar and tapioca pearls, and have called for greater regulation of the industry. In addition, there have been reports of poor working conditions in some Bubble Tea factories, which has led to calls for greater transparency and accountability.

Despite these challenges, Bubble Tea remains a beloved drink around the world. It is a drink that has brought people together, and has become a symbol of Taiwanese culture and identity. As the global food and beverage industry continues to evolve, it is clear that Bubble Tea will remain a major player in this space for years to come.

Bubble Tea is more than just a drink; it is a cultural phenomenon that has captured the hearts and minds of people around the world. From its humble beginnings in Taiwan in the 1980s, Bubble Tea has grown into a global industry, generating billions of dollars in revenue each year.

The cultural significance of Bubble Tea in Taiwan cannot be overstated. It is a drink that has become a symbol of Taiwanese identity, and has brought people together in a way that few other things can. It is a testament to the creativity and ingenuity of the Taiwanese people, and has helped to put Taiwan on the map as a leader in the food and beverage industry.

As the popularity of Bubble Tea continues to grow around the world, it is important to remember the cultural significance of this drink. It is more than just a trend or a fad; it is a drink that represents a rich and vibrant culture, and has the power to bring people together in a way that few other things can.

Top Places to Visit in Taiwan

Taiwan is a stunning destination that offers a diverse mix of natural wonders, vibrant cities, cultural sites, and culinary delights. From towering mountains to pristine beaches, Taiwan has something for everyone. Here are some of the top places to visit in Taiwan:

1. Taipei

Taipei, Taiwan's dynamic capital city, is a cultural, historical, and modern melting pot. Taipei has something for everyone, from towering skyscrapers to calm temples, lively night markets to tranquil parks. I may not be able to physically visit the city with you as a language model, but I can surely take you on a virtual tour of this intriguing place.

Let's start with the city's history and culture before diving into the city's attractions and must-see sites. Taipei's origins may be traced back to the 18th century, when it was known as Tamsui, a modest commercial town. When the Qing Dynasty established Taiwan as a province of China in the nineteenth century, the city's name was changed to Taipei. Taipei saw substantial development and modernisation during Japan's colonization of Taiwan from 1895 to 1945.

The city was extensively damaged during WWII, but it was rebuilt thereafter. Taipei is now a vibrant and lively metropolis with a distinct blend of traditional Chinese culture and modern influences.

Taipei 101, a 508-meter-tall skyscraper, is one of the city's most recognizable sights. The structure was previously the highest in the world and is still the tallest green building in the world, thanks to sustainable features like rainwater recycling and energy-efficient technology. A high-speed elevator takes visitors to the summit, where they may enjoy panoramic views of the city.

The National Palace Museum, which holds one of the world's most significant collections of Chinese art and antiques, is another must-see destination. The museum's collection contains about 700,000 ancient Chinese imperial relics, calligraphy, paintings, and pottery, some of which date back over 5,000 years.

Taipei offers some lovely temples worth visiting for those wanting a more spiritual experience. Longshan Temple, in the Wanhua area, is one of the city's oldest and most well-known temples, going back to the 18th century. The temple is devoted to a variety of deities, including Guanyin, the goddess of mercy, and it is decorated with beautiful carvings, bright paintings, and traditional architecture.

The Ximending area, recognized as the city's young cultural centre, is one of Taipei's most unusual attractions. There are many stores, boutiques, and street sellers in the neighborhood, as well as cinemas, theaters, and performance venues. The boisterous environment of Ximending is ideal for anyone searching for a taste of Taipei's vibrant street culture.

Taipei offers various wonderful parks to explore for individuals who like outdoor activities. Yangmingshan National Park, located just outside of town, is a sprawling park featuring hiking paths, hot springs, and picturesque overlooks. The park also has a diverse flora and fauna, including cherry blossoms, azaleas, and unique bird species.

One of my favorite memories of Taipei is visiting the Shilin Night Market in the Shilin neighborhood. The night market is a hive of activity, with sellers selling anything from street food to souvenirs. I recall being overwhelmed by the market's sights, noises, and scents, as well as the sheer amount of people. It was a sensory onslaught, but in the greatest manner conceivable. I wandered around the market for hours, eating various Taiwanese specialties including stinky tofu, oyster omelets, and bubble tea. I also got the opportunity to participate in activities and win prizes, which added to the pleasure.

I chose to visit some of Taipei's calmer and more tranquil places after indulging in the great street food and activities at the night market. The Taipei Confucius Temple, located in the Datong area, piqued my interest. The temple was a quiet oasis in the center of the city, dedicated to the famed Chinese philosopher Confucius. The temple complex had classic Chinese buildings, lovely gardens, and peaceful ponds stocked with koi fish. I spent some time enjoying the rich features of the temple's beautiful decorations and reflecting on Confucius' teachings.

I made my way to Taipei's famed Taipei 101 tower as the day changed to darkness. I rode the high-speed elevator to the top of the skyscraper and gazed out the window at the spectacular view of the city skyline. Taipei's lights twinkled like stars, and I was struck by the enormous size of the city. I felt like I was on top of the world when standing on the observation deck.

The combination of old and new, traditional and modern,

was one of the things that struck me about Taipei. On the one hand, there are old temples and relics that have stood the test of time. On the other hand, you have towering buildings, cutting-edge technology, and a never-sleeping metropolis. Taipei is a city that embraces both its past and its future, which makes it a one-of-a-kind and intriguing destination.

As my stay in Taipei drew to an end, I realized there was still so much more to see and do. Taipei has something for everyone, from the bustling street culture of Ximending to the quiet serenity of Yangmingshan National Park. Taipei has something for everyone, whether you're a foodie, a history lover, or an adventure seeker.

Taipei will steal your heart and leave you with memories that will last a lifetime. Its distinct combination of culture, history, and modernity distinguishes it as a one-of-a-kind destination. So, what are you holding out for? Come see Taipei for yourself and learn about all this great city has to offer.

2. Kaohsiung

Kaohsiung, located in southwestern Taiwan, is the country's third-largest city after Taipei and New Taipei. It is regarded as Taiwan's industrial capital, but it is also a city with a rich cultural past and a dynamic environment, making it a must-see destination for visitors. Kaohsiung is a city that combines the old and the contemporary, with historic temples and shrines coexisting alongside modern skyscrapers and commercial malls. In this post, I will look at some of the best attractions and activities to do in Kaohsiung and take you on a tour of this lovely city.

The Lotus Pond, a man-made lake in the Zuoying District, is one of Kaohsiung's most famous attractions. The Lotus Pond is well-known for the numerous temples and pagodas that dot the lake's banks. When visiting the Lotus Pond, you must view the Dragon and Tiger Pagodas. These colorful pagodas are said to offer good luck to guests who arrive by the dragon's mouth and escape through the tiger's mouth. The Confucius Temple, Taiwan's largest Confucian temple, is another famous sight on the Lotus Pond.

Another site not to be missed is the Fo Guang Shan Buddha Museum. It is the world's largest Buddhist museum and home to a colossal Buddha statue that rises 108 meters tall. Visitors can wander around the museum's many display halls, which feature Buddhist art, history, and philosophy.

The Pier-2 Art Center, a creative and cultural hub located in the Yancheng District, is one of Kaohsiung's distinctive attractions. The Pier-2 Art Center is a repurposed warehouse that has been turned into a dynamic art environment complete with galleries, studios, cafés, and stores. Visitors may explore the complex's diverse art installations and murals, as well as engage in seminars and events.

Kaohsiung is also known for its night markets, the most prominent of which is the Liuhe Night Market. It is located in the Sinsing District and is home to a plethora of food booths and merchants serving a wide range of Taiwanese street cuisine. Oyster omelets, stinky tofu, and bubble tea are among the must-try foods.

The Kaohsiung Museum of Fine Arts, the largest art museum in southern Taiwan, is also worth a visit. The museum houses a broad collection of paintings, sculptures, and installations by Taiwanese and international artists.

Aside from these top attractions, Kaohsiung boasts a number of lovely parks and green areas. Central Park, located in the Lingya District, is one of the most prominent. It is a popular place for folks to exercise, relax, and appreciate nature. There is also a lake, a playground, and a small zoo in the park.

After breakfast, I go to the Fo Guang Shan Buddha Museum, which is perched on a cliff overlooking the city. I rode the cable car up to the museum, marveling at the breathtaking views of the city below. I examined the many display halls of the museum and learned about Buddhist art and philosophy.

I go to the Pier-2 Art Center in the afternoon to immerse myself in the city's creative and cultural atmosphere. I go throughout the complex, appreciating the paintings and street art on the walls. I took part in a session and made my own work of art to take home as a keepsake.

As the sun sets, I make my way to the Liuhe Night Market to sample some Taiwanese street cuisine. The scents of excellent cuisine fill the air as I go through the stalls. I ate some oyster omelets, stinky tofu, and drank some delicious bubble tea.

The next day, I began my day by browsing the galleries and appreciating the artwork at the Kaohsiung Museum of Fine Arts. I learn about Taiwan's art history and get a greater respect for the country's culture and creativity.

In the afternoon, I go to Central Park for a leisurely stroll and to breathe in some fresh air. I wandered around the lake, admiring the ducks and swans. I came to the playground to watch the kids play and have a lunch on the grass.

As night falls, I make my way to the Love River, which is noted for its romantic environment. I took a boat trip along the river, appreciating the city lights and the water's reflections. I rested and took in the city's splendor.

As my journey concludes, I reflect on my stay in Kaohsiung. I've experienced the city's culture, creativity, and natural beauty, and I've created memories that last a lifetime. I've gained a new appreciation for Taiwan and the great places it has to offer.

3. Sun Moon Lake

Sun Moon Lake is one of Taiwan's most beautiful and gorgeous locations. Sun Moon Lake, located in Taiwan's central mountain range, is a must-see location for anybody who appreciates spectacular natural scenery, tranquil settings, and cultural legacy. The lake is surrounded by lush green hills, towering mountains, and a serene environment, making it a great site for rest and reflection.

The lake itself, a body of crystal-clear water that shimmers in the sunshine, is at the center of Sun Moon Lake. The lake's name comes from the fact that it is fashioned like a sun on one side and a crescent moon on the other. Fresh mountain streams feed the lake's deep blue waters, while the surrounding forests and hills provide a natural home for a broad diversity of flora and wildlife.

Several indigenous tribes dwell in the Sun Moon Lake area and have done so for millennia. These tribes have their own distinct rituals, traditions, and cultures that have been passed down through the decades. Visitors may learn about the local culture and history by visiting the area's various museums and cultural institutions.

Cycling around Sun Moon Lake is one of the most popular activities. The beautiful road around the lake is around 30 kilometers long and provides breathtaking views of the surrounding mountains, woods, and lake. The road is also densely packed with restaurants, cafés, and souvenir stores, making it an ideal day excursion for travelers.

A boat trip around Sun Moon Lake is a terrific way to explore the lake. Boats of many varieties are available, including tour boats, pedal boats, and electric boats. Each boat provides a distinct view of the lake and its surroundings. Visitors may also take a cable car journey to the summit of adjacent mountains for panoramic views of the lake and surrounding region.

The Wenwu Temple is one of the most intriguing spots to visit in Sun Moon Lake. The temple is dedicated to Confucius and two other Chinese deities and is located on the north side of the lake. The temple is a stunning example of traditional Chinese architecture, and the surrounding gardens and courtyards offer a serene haven.

The Sun Moon Lake National Scenic Area Administration Office is a fantastic place to start if you want to learn more about the region's history. The office contains a variety of information on the area's history, culture, and natural resources, as well as information on the numerous activities and attractions.

Sun Moon Lake visitors may also engage in a variety of

outdoor activities such as hiking, fishing, and kayaking. Visitors may rent fishing equipment and try their luck at capturing some of the lake's fish, which include tilapia, carp, and bass. The surrounding hills and mountains are also suitable for trekking, with a variety of pathways for hikers of all skill levels.

Sun Moon Lake is well-known for its superb cuisine, in addition to its natural beauty and cultural legacy. The region is well-known for its tea farms, and tourists may sample some of the world's greatest teas. Traditional Taiwanese foods such as beef noodle soup, braised pig belly, and stinky tofu may also be found in the region.

I chose to go to Sun Moon Lake on a wonderful summer day. I'd heard so much about this breathtaking natural beauty, and I couldn't wait to see it for myself. I came to the lake early in the morning to see the crystal-clear waters glistening in the sunlight.

I took a great breath of the pure mountain air as I stood on the coast, feeling the cold breeze against my face. I knew I was in for an incredible adventure.

I decided to go boating on the lake, and I rented a pedal

boat so that I could take my time and enjoy the sights at my own leisure. I was fascinated by the beauty of my surroundings as I pedaled around the lake. The serene ambience provided by the lush green hills, towering mountains, and deep blue waters of the lake put me at rest.

I was biking along when I observed a bunch of fisherman casting their hooks into the sea. I piloted my boat closer to them, curious, and started up a discussion. They were polite and kind, and they showed me some of the fish they had caught that day. I could smell the fresh fish and considered asking if they could prepare any for me, but I decided to continue my expedition and explore more of the lake.

As I pedaled, I noticed a cable car soaring over the lake and knew I wanted to ride it. I strolled over to the cable car station and bought a ticket for the journey after docking my pedal boat. The cable car carried me to the summit of a neighboring mountain, where I was met with breathtaking views of the lake and surrounding mountains. I paused for a few moments to take in the scenery before returning to the lake.

I noticed signage for the Wenwu Temple while hiking and knew I had to there. The temple was a stunning example of traditional Chinese construction, with detailed carvings and vibrant ornamentation. Before continuing on my tour, I spent some time exploring the temple and learning about its history.

I decided to take a leisurely stroll around the lake as the sun began to drop. The cold evening wind was nice, and I appreciated the lake's tranquil ambience. As I traveled, I noticed various restaurants and cafés and chose to dine there. I ordered several typical Taiwanese meals and was pleasantly surprised by the exquisite flavors and scents.

I knew as I completed my supper that my experience at Sun Moon Lake had come to an end. As I drove away from the lake, I felt sad because I knew I would miss the natural beauty, cultural legacy, and pleasant people I had met during my vacation. But I also knew that I'd never forget the incredible journey I'd had in Sun Moon Lake, and that I'd always treasure the memories I'd made there.

4. Kenting National Park

Kenting National Park is a real Taiwanese treasure, with beautiful natural landscapes, rich cultural attractions, and thrilling outdoor activities for people of all ages. Kenting National Park, located in the southernmost portion of Taiwan, is a popular destination for travelers from all over the world looking to see the island's rich cultural and natural history. Kenting National Park, with its towering mountains and crystal blue waterways, is a must-see location for anybody who enjoys adventure, beauty, and the great outdoors.

Kenting National Park's history extends back to the late nineteenth century, when the region was used as a hunting site by the Japanese during their colonization of Taiwan. The Japanese colonial administration constructed the Kenting Forest Recreation Area in 1935, which became a favorite retreat for Japanese officials and their families. The park was taken up by the Taiwanese government after WWII and was formally declared as Kenting National Park in 1984.

Kenting National Park is currently famous for its breathtaking beauty, diversified animals, and cultural attractions. The park is home to approximately 1,200 plant species, 305 bird species, and 101 animal species, making it a paradise for naturc lovcrs and wildlife aficionados. With their brilliant blue seas, immaculate white sand, and spectacular sunsets, the park's beaches are also a popular destination.

The Kenting Night Market is one of the most popular attractions in Kenting National Park. The night market, located in the middle of the park, is a vibrant and busy hub of activity where visitors can try a broad range of local cuisines, purchase for souvenirs, and watch live performances by street performers. The market is open every night and is an excellent location to learn about local culture and food.

The Eluanbi Lighthouse is another must-see item in Kenting National Park. The lighthouse, located near Taiwan's southernmost tip, provides beautiful views of the surrounding ocean and is a favorite place for sunset viewing. Visitors may also visit Eluanbi Park, which has a number of picturesque paths that go through lush woods and past magnificent views.

Kenting National Park provides a broad range of outdoor activities, including hiking, snorkeling, diving, surfing, and windsurfing. Hiking paths in the park range from simple to difficult, providing possibilities for all fitness levels. Snorkeling and diving are popular activities in the park's crystal-clear waters, which are home to a diverse range of colorful fish and other marine life. Surfing and windsurfing are other popular water sports, with waves ideal for both novice and expert surfers.

Renting a scooter or bicycle is one of the greatest methods to explore Kenting National Park. The park is a terrific spot to explore on two wheels, with its winding lanes and picturesque panoramas. Visitors may hire a scooter or bicycle from one of the park's many rental shops and then go on their own journey. The park also has a variety of tiny villages and towns where tourists may eat or shop at the local markets.

My visit to Kenting National Park was a wonderful experience for me. I'd always heard good things about the park's natural beauty and cultural attractions, and I couldn't wait to see them for myself. On a lovely day in early summer, I entered the park and felt the warm sea wind on my face.

My first trip was the Kenting Night Market, where I spent hours browsing the vendors, enjoying local cuisine, and watching street entertainers. The aromas of sizzling meat and spices filled the air, while music and laughing filled the room. Everything from grilled squid to steamed buns was on the menu, and I even risked the famed stinky tofu. The night market was a sensory overload, and I left feeling happy and content.

I hired a scooter the next morning and headed out to explore the park's picturesque roads and hiking paths. My first visit was in the Shedding Nature Park, where I climbed through deep forests and past huge waterfalls. The scenery was stunning, with misty mountains and emerald green valley’s reaching as far as the eye could see. As I breathed in the pure mountain air and listened to the sound of the running river, I felt a sense of serenity and tranquility come over me.

I was eager for some beach time after a few hours of trekking. I hopped on my scooter and headed down to Nanwan Beach, one of the park's most popular beaches, where I spent the day relaxing on the sand and swimming in the crystal blue ocean. The beach was full yet tranquil, with families and friends relaxing in the sun and waves.

I took my scooter to the Eluanbi Lighthouse as the sun began to set to catch the sunset. The sights were breathtaking, with the sunset's orange and pink colours coloring the sky and the water. I felt grateful and amazement for the natural beauty surrounding me as I watched the sun gently sink beyond the horizon.

The next day, I decided to give surfing a try. I hired a surfboard and wetsuit from one of the park's surf shops and went to Jialeshui Beach, one of the top surf areas in the vicinity. The waves were ideal for first-timers like me, and I spent the morning surfing them and soaking up the rays.

I spent the afternoon exploring Hengchun Old Town, a wonderful historic quarter that was once a bustling commerce centre. I strolled through the small streets, appreciating the brightly colored houses and medieval architecture. I also went to the Hengchun Gate, which is the sole surviving city gate from the old Hengchun city wall. The gate represented the town's long history and cultural richness.

As my visit to Kenting National Park came to a conclusion, I was thankful for the experiences and memories I had made. In every aspect, the park exceeded my expectations, providing a great combination of natural beauty, cultural activities, and outdoor activity. I departed with amazement and astonishment for the natural environment, as well as a renewed understanding for Taiwanese culture's depth and diversity.

5. Tainan

Tainan is a city located in Taiwan's southern area. Tainan, Taiwan's oldest city, has a population of around 1.8 million people and has played an essential part in the country's history, culture, and economics. In this post, I will look at Tainan's rich history, colorful culture, and delectable cuisine, as well as give an appealing narrative on how to visit this intriguing city.

Tainan's history may be traced back to the 17th century, when it was known as "Tayouan" by the Dutch colonizers of Taiwan. Koxinga, a Ming dynasty supporter, eventually seized the city and created the Kingdom of Tungning in 1661. Tainan was Taiwan's capital during the Qing era and an important hub for trade, culture, and politics.

The Anping Tree House, which was once a warehouse erected by the Dutch in the 17th century, is one of Tainan's most recognizable sites. The structure was eventually abandoned and taken over by banyan trees, producing a one-of-a-kind and breathtaking scene. Visitors may tour the tree home, learn about its history, and take in the breathtaking view.

The Chihkan Tower, commonly known as the Fort Provintia, is another must-see historical sight in Tainan. The tower, built by the Dutch in the 17th century, operated as a stronghold and administrative headquarters under the Qing dynasty. Visitors may now tour the tower and learn about its history and significance, as well as see the exquisite architecture and gardens that surround it.

Tainan's strong culture is evident in its art, music, and festivals. The Taiwan Lantern Festival, which takes place every February, is one of Tainan's most popular celebrations. The event attracts tourists from all across Taiwan and beyond with its colorful lanterns, entertainment, and cuisine.

The National Museum of Taiwan Literature, which is committed to conserving and promoting Taiwan's literary legacy, is another cultural destination in Tainan. Exhibits on prominent Taiwanese writers and their works, as well as interactive displays and activities for visitors of all ages, are availablc at thc muscum.

Tainan is particularly well-known for its tasty cuisine, which represents the city's history and cultural influences. Danzi noodles, which are handmade and served with a variety of toppings such as minced pork, bamboo shoots, and bean sprouts, are one of Tainan's most popular meals. The oyster omelet, which consists of a crispy omelet packed with juicy oysters and topped with a sweet and salty sauce, is another must-try meal in Tainan.

Tainan's hidden jewels and local favorites are essential for experiencing the city's beauty. One option is to take a guided tour, such as the one provided by Tainan Cultural Heritage Tour. Visitors will be taken to some of Tainan's most prominent locations, as well as secret temples, street markets, and food vendors.

Visitors may learn about Tainan's history, culture, and food, as well as engage with residents and immerse themselves in the city's colorful environment, throughout the trip. A visit to a traditional tea shop, where tourists may sample many varieties of Taiwanese tea and learn about its history and significance, is one of the tour's highlights.

As the sun sets, the trip brings tourists to the Grand Matsu Temple, one of Tainan's most magnificent and historic temples. Visitors may observe residents praying and performing rituals while also admiring the gorgeous building and exquisite decorations.

After visiting the temple, the trip takes travelers to a local street market where they may sample some of Tainan's famed street cuisine. The market has a broad variety of excellent and economical alternatives, ranging from crispy fried chicken to savory pork buns.

The trip continues into the night, taking tourists to a local pub or night market where they may continue to see Tainan's thriving nightlife and meet new people. The tour guide makes suggestions for beverages and nibbles, as well as suggestions for travelling around the city and enjoying its distinct culture.

Overall, having a guided tour of Tainan is a nice opportunity to learn about the city's rich history, vibrant culture, and exquisite food. Tainan has something for everyone, whether you're a first-time tourist or a seasoned traveler. So, why not start your Tainan journey by booking a tour today?

6. Taichung

Taiwan is a lovely East Asian island nation noted for its colorful culture, great cuisine, and breathtaking natural landscape. Taichung, a busy metropolis in the island's center, is one of Taiwan's most interesting cities. Taichung is a city full of surprises, with a fascinating history, intriguing culture, and wonderful treasures just waiting to be discovered.

Taichung has a long history that dates back to the 17th century, when it was founded by Chinese immigrants. The city has expanded and changed over the years, becoming a hub for trade, business, and culture. Taichung is now a vibrant, contemporary metropolis with a population of about 2.8 million people.

Taichung's architecture is one of its most notable features. The National Taichung Theater, created by famous Japanese architect Toyo Ito, is one of the city's most notable structures. This magnificent edifice has a futuristic design with undulating curves and a roof that appears to be a large piece of cloth stretched over the structure. The Rainbow camp, a former military camp that has been turned into a colorful and dynamic community owing to the efforts of a local artist named Huang Yung-Fu, is another must-see architectural wonder in Taichung.

Of course, no trip to Taichung would be complete without seeing some of its magnificent temples. There are several exquisite temples in the city, including the Wanhe Temple, the Paochueh Temple, and the Taichung Confucius Temple. These temples are not only breathtakingly gorgeous, but they are also significant cultural landmarks that provide insight into Taiwan's rich history and traditions.

Exploring Taichung by bike is one of the greatest ways to do so. The city offers a well-developed bicycle network, with bike lanes and routes that lead you through some of the most charming districts and scenic sites in the city. Renting a bike is simple and inexpensive, and it's a terrific way to see the city at your own leisure.

Why not try hot air ballooning in Taichung for a one-of-a-kind and unforgettable experience? Taichung is one of the few sites in Taiwan where you may go on a hot air balloon flight, and it's an unforgettable experience. You'll enjoy a bird's eye view of Taichung's breathtaking environment, from rolling hills and green woods to glittering rivers and lakes, as you soar far above the city.

Walking is another excellent method to see Taichung. The Taichung Metropolitan Park, the Houfeng Bikeway, and the Dongshi Forest Garden are among the city's many lovely parks and gardens. These green parks provide a calm escape from the city's hustle and bustle, and they're an excellent spot to rest and unwind.

Taichung is a foodie's heaven. The city is well-known for its delectable cuisine, which combines traditional Taiwanese delicacies with modern fusion cuisine. Taichung has something for everyone's taste, from street cuisine to high-end eateries. Braised pork rice, beef noodle soup, and bubble tea, which was originated in Taiwan, are all must-tries.

Let me now tell you about my own exploration of Taichung. I had always wanted to visit Taiwan, so when the opportunity offered, I seized it. I opted to begin my journey in Taichung because I had heard so many good things about the city.

The first thing I did was rent a bike and ride around the city. I began in Taichung Metropolitan Park, a huge green park with a lake, a playground, and a variety of picturesque pathways. From there, I rode my bike through some of Taichung's residential areas, appreciating the traditional architecture and the gorgeous gardens that lined the streets.

Next, I went to Rainbow Village, which was unquestionably one of the highlights of my vacation. I was amazed by the brilliant colors and colorful motifs that adorned every surface of the hamlet as soon as I arrived. The artist who changed the town, Huang Yung-Fu, was on hand to welcome tourists and give them a tour of his magnificent work. He described the history of the community and the inspiration for his work as he walked us around.

I continued my bike journey beyond Rainbow Village to the Paochueh Temple, a gorgeous temple with complex sculptures, bright paintings, and beautiful gardens. The temple was crowded with devotees, and the air was thick with the aroma of incense. I wandered into the temple, appreciating the art and architecture and absorbing in the tranquil ambience.

I went to one of Taichung's famed night markets for lunch, which are a must-see for any foodie. I sampled everything from warm bowls of noodles to grilled skewers of meat and veggies. And, of course, I had to sample some bubble tea, which was the ideal refreshing drink to wash down all of the food.

I had a hot air balloon flight over the city in the afternoon, which was a fantastic experience. The beauty of Taichung from above as we hovered high above the buildings and streets astounded me. We flew through lush woods and dazzling lakes, and even received a sight of the distant mountains.

Finally, I finished my day at the National Taichung Theater, which was a work of art in and of it. The building's distinctive and useful design included places for concerts, exhibits, and workshops. That evening, I went to a performance there and was blown away by the acoustics and the caliber of the singers.

Overall, I had a fantastic experience in Taichung. The city was full of surprises, and I had a great time finding all of its hidden gems. There was something fresh and intriguing around every bend, from the vibrant Rainbow Village to the serene Paochueh Temple. And, of course, the meal was fantastic. I would strongly suggest Taichung to anybody seeking a one-of-a-kind and spectacular vacation experience.

7. Hualien

Hualien is a picturesque city on Taiwan's eastern coast. It is well-known for its breathtaking natural beauty, diverse cultural heritage, and delectable gastronomy. The city is surrounded by beautiful mountains and the Pacific Ocean, providing guests with a one-of-a-kind and amazing experience. I will look at the main attractions, activities, and things to do in Hualien in this post.

Because of its distant position and pure natural surroundings, Hualien is sometimes referred to as Taiwan's "backyard." Several national parks are located in the city, notably Taroko National Park, which is a must-see for anybody visiting Hualien. Taroko National Park, with its towering cliffs, lush woods, deep gorges, and crystal-clear rivers, is one of Taiwan's most attractive national parks. Hiking, camping, and river rafting are among the activities available to tourists in the park. The Taroko Gorge, a 19-kilometer-long gorge cut out of the marble by the Liwu River, is the park's showpiece. The gorge is stunning, with towering cliffs and flowing waterfalls.

Qingshui Cliff, a 21-kilometer-long stretch of coastline with spectacular views of the Pacific Ocean, is another renowned destination in Hualien. The gorgeous Su-Hua Highway connects Hualien and Yilan, and the cliff is located on it. The route is famous for its twisting turns, spectacular scenery, and difficult driving conditions. Visitors may take in the breathtaking view by stopping at many lookout sites along the journey.

Exploring Hualien on bike is one of the greatest ways to do so. There are various bike rental shops in the city that provide a variety of bikes, from regular cycles to mountain bikes. Throughout the city, there are various bike lanes that transport tourists to some of Hualien's most stunning natural sites. The Hualien Bike Trail, a 15-kilometer-long bike trail that connects Hualien City to the Pacific Ocean, is one of the most popular biking routes. The hike provides breathtaking views of the ocean and adjacent mountains.

Hualien features various museums and cultural facilities for individuals interested in history and culture, providing a look into Taiwan's rich cultural legacy. The Hualien Cultural Creative Industries Park, built in a former winery, is one of the most popular museums. Visitors may buy handcrafted goods, ceramics, and textiles at the park, which features the work of local artists and artisans. The Pine Garden, a historic Japanese colonial home that has been refurbished and transformed into an art museum, is another famous sight. The museum shows local artists' work as well as exhibits on Taiwan's history and culture.

The option to engage in a tribal tour is one of the most unique experiences in Hualien. Several indigenous tribes live in Hualien, including the Amis, Atayal, and Bunun. Visitors can take a tour of a typical tribal village and learn about the indigenous people's customs, traditions, and way of life. The excursions often include a visit to a tribal museum, a traditional dance performance, and a traditional cuisine taste.

Hiking is one of the finest methods to appreciate Hualien's natural beauty. There are various hiking paths in the city, ranging from simple to difficult. The Shakadang route, a 4.5-kilometer-long route that brings tourists into the Taroko Gorge, is one of the most popular. The route is quite straightforward and provides breathtaking views of the Liwu River and neighboring mountains. The Zhuilu Old trek, a tough 10-kilometer-long trek with breathtaking views of the Taroko Gorge and the Pacific Ocean, is another popular hike.

Outdoor adventure in Taiwan

Taiwan is a tiny island country located off the coast of China. It is a veritable treasure trove of outdoor experiences, ranging from challenging mountain excursions to relaxed beach bike tours. Because of the island's varied landscape, it is a favorite destination for adventurers from all over the world.

In this guide, I will look at some of Taiwan's top outdoor experiences as well as the most popular locations for those adventures.

Hiking

Hiking is one of Taiwan's most popular outdoor hobbies, and for good reason. The island is home to numerous spectacular mountain ranges, notably the Central Mountain Range, which runs along the middle of Taiwan and has several 3,000-meter-tall peaks.

Taroko Gorge National Park, located on the island's east coast, is one of the most popular trekking locations in Taiwan. The Zhuilu Old Trail, a tiny cliffside trail with spectacular views of the canyon below, is one of the park's most difficult walks. The park also has numerous beautiful waterfalls, including the Baiyang Waterfall, which can be reached by a short, simple climb.

Yushan National Park, which has Taiwan's tallest mountain, Yushan, is another famous hiking destination. The mountain is 3,952 meters high and provides a difficult but rewarding walk to the peak. The park also has a number of additional hiking paths, including the Batongguan Trail, which provides breathtaking views of the surrounding mountains.

Cycling

Cycling is a popular outdoor sport in Taiwan, due to the island's well-kept bike trails and attractive coastline routes. The East Coast Scenic Area, which spans for about 170 kilometers along Taiwan's east coast, is one of the most popular cycling destinations in Taiwan.

The route passes through beautiful coastal scenery, including rocky cliffs and sandy beaches. It also travels through numerous attractive little towns and fishing villages, providing an excellent opportunity to learn about the local culture.

Sun Moon Lake Scenic Area, located in central Taiwan, is another famous riding destination. A 33-kilometer cycling trail around the lake and provides spectacular views of the neighboring mountains. Other attractions in the area include the Wenwu Temple and the Formosan Aboriginal Culture Village.

Rock Climbing

Taiwan's rough mountain ranges and limestone cliffs make it a popular location for rock climbers. Long Dong, on Taiwan's northeast coast, is one of the most popular rock climbing places.

There are approximately 600 climbing routes in the region, ranging from beginner to intermediate, and the scenery is breathtaking. It also has a number of marine caverns that may be explored by kayak or stand-up paddleboard.

Baishawan, in northern Taiwan, is another renowned rock climbing site. Several limestone cliffs, including the famed Mushroom Rock, provide tough routes for expert climbers.

Surfing

Taiwan's vast coastline and steady waves make it a popular surfing destination. Jinzun, located on the island's east coast, is one of the most popular surfing spots in Taiwan.

A long, sandy beach with steady waves is available in the vicinity, making it ideal for both novice and expert surfers. It also has a number of surf schools and rental businesses, making it simple for tourists to get started.

Jialeshui, in southern Taiwan, is another renowned surfing spot. The location is famed for its tremendous waves, which may reach a height of four meters. It's a popular choice for experienced surfers searching for a new challenge.

Shopping in Taiwan

Taiwan is a busy East Asian island country that provides travellers with a one-of-a-kind shopping experience. Taiwan provides something for every style of consumer, from retail malls to street markets. In this guide, I will look at the numerous shopping opportunities in Taiwan, including souvenirs and presents for travellers.

Souvenirs and Gifts in Taiwan

When it comes to souvenirs and presents, Taiwan has a rich and varied culture that provides travelers with a choice of possibilities. Here are some of the top souvenirs and presents available in Taiwan.

Tea

Taiwan is well-known for its tea culture, and it produces some of the world's greatest teas. Oolong tea, which has a sweet and flowery taste, is the most popular form of tea in Taiwan. In Taiwan, other popular teas include black tea, green tea, and white tea. Tea stores may be found all around Taiwan, and they sell a range of teas in various tastes and containers. A box of high-quality Taiwanese tea is an ideal keepsake or present for tea enthusiasts.

Taiwanese Snacks

Taiwanese snacks are well-known around the globe for their distinct tastes and textures. Taiwanese delicacies popular include pineapple cakes, sun cakes, mochi, and beef jerky. These treats are available in local markets and souvenir stores. They are often offered in gift boxes or individually wrapped bundles, making them convenient to travel and carry.

Taiwanese Art and Crafts

Taiwanese art and crafts are distinctive, reflecting the country's diverse culture and history. Pottery, woodcarvings, and calligraphy are among the most prominent Taiwanese crafts. These crafts may be found at local markets and souvenir stores, and they make an ideal present or house decoration.

Jade Jewelry

Jade is a valuable precious stone in Chinese culture. Taiwan makes some of the world's greatest jade jewelry, which can be found in local markets and jewelry stores. Because jade is said to bring good luck and wealth, it is a favorite gift among Taiwanese people.

Shopping Malls in Taiwan

Taiwan features some of Asia's most contemporary and opulent retail complexes. These shopping centers include a diverse selection of merchandise, including high-end clothes, electronics, and cosmetics. Here are some of Taiwan's greatest retail complexes.

Taipei 101 Mall

The landmark Taipei 101 structure, which was formerly the highest building in the world, houses the Taipei 101 Mall. Over 500 retailers are located in the mall, including premium fashion labels such as Gucci, Louis Vuitton, and Chanel. Taipei 101 Mall also has some of Taipei's greatest restaurants, serving a wide range of international cuisines.

Shin Kong Mitsukoshi

Shin Kong Mitsukoshi is Taiwan's biggest and most popular department store. The shop has many locations in Taiwan, including Taipei, Taichung, and Kaohsiung. Clothing, cosmetics, electronics, and household appliances are among the items available at the establishments.

Breeze Center

Breeze Center is a luxury retail complex in Taipei. Over

300 retailers are located in the mall, including major names such as Burberry, Dior, and Hermès. Breeze Center also has some of Taipei's greatest restaurants, providing both local and foreign cuisine.

Taiwanese Street Markets

Street markets are an indelible aspect of Taiwanese culture, providing a diverse choice of goods at reasonable costs. These markets are vivid and colorful, and they provide travellers with a one-of-a-kind shopping experience. Here are some of Taiwan's top street markets.

Night Market in Shilin

Shilin Night Market is Taipei's biggest and most popular night market. Over 500 food and shop vendors provide a wide range of Taiwanese street cuisine, apparel, accessories, and souvenirs. At the market, popular items to sample include stinky tofu, fried chicken steak, and bubble tea.

Night Market on Raohe Street

Another renowned night market in Taipei is Raohe Street Night Market. Traditional Taiwanese appetizers and local specialties like as pork pepper buns, oyster omelets, and shaved ice desserts are popular at the market. The market also features a section devoted to apparel and accessories, making it an excellent destination for souvenir shopping.

Night Market in Liuhe

Liuhe Night Market is a must-see for seafood enthusiasts. The market, which is situated in Kaohsiung, is well-known for its fresh seafood kiosks, which provide a range of meals such as grilled squid, shrimp soup, and seafood noodles. The market also features an area for souvenir shopping, where you may buy local handicrafts, apparel, and accessories.

Shopping in Taiwan is a one-of-a-kind and unforgettable experience that every visitor should attempt. The country's shopping opportunities are diverse, including contemporary retail malls and bustling street markets. Tourists may also purchase souvenirs and presents reflecting Taiwan's rich culture and history, such as tea, food, art and crafts, and jade jewelry. Taiwan offers enough to offer any sort of consumer, whether they are shopping for premium brands or inexpensive souvenirs.

Useful Taiwan vocabulary and phrases

Taiwan is a fascinating destination with a rich cultural heritage, stunning natural landscapes, and a bustling modern cityscape. Whether you are traveling to Taiwan for business or pleasure, it's always helpful to know some basic phrases and vocabulary to help you get around and communicate with locals. In this guide I will cover some essential phrases and vocabulary related to basic communication, food and drink, transportation, and emergencies in Taiwan.

Basic Phrases

Greetings: When meeting someone for the first time, it's customary to greet them by saying "nǐ hǎo" which means "hello." If you want to be more polite, you can say "nín hǎo" instead. If you are leaving, you can say "zàijiàn" which means "goodbye."

Thank You: If someone does something for you or gives you something, it's polite to say "xièxiè" which means "thank you." If you want to be more formal, you can say "dàjiā hǎo kèqì" which means "thank you, everyone, for your kindness."

Excuse Me: If you need to get someone's attention or ask for something, you can say "duìbuqǐ" which means "excuse me" or "sorry."

Yes and No: In Mandarin Chinese, "yes" is "shì" and "no" is "bù shì" . However, in Taiwan, people often use "hǎo" to mean "yes" and "bù hǎo" to mean "no."

Food and Drink Vocabulary

Taiwan is famous for its delicious cuisine, which includes a wide variety of dishes from traditional street food to upscale fine dining. Here are some essential food and drink vocabulary words to help you navigate the local cuisine:

Rice: "mǐfàn"
Noodles: "miàn tiáo"
Soup: "tāng"
Meat: "ròu"
Seafood: "hǎixiān"
Vegetables: "shūcài"
Fruit: "shuǐguǒ"

Tea: "chá"

Coffee: "kāfēi"

Beer: "píjiǔ"

Wine: "hóngjiǔ"

Water: "shuǐ"

When ordering food, you can use the phrase "wǒ yào" to mean "I want" and then specify the dish or drink you want. For example, if you want to order a bowl of beef noodle soup, you can say "wǒ yào niúròu miàn tiáo tāng"

Transportation Vocabulary

Getting around Taiwan is relatively easy thanks to its modern public transportation system. Here are some essential transportation vocabulary words to help you get around:

Bus: "gōnggòng qìchē"

MRT: "dìtiě"

Train: "huǒchē

Taxi: "chūzū chē"

Airport: "jīchǎng"

Train station: "huǒchē zhàn"

Bus stop: "gōnggòng qìchē zhàn"l

Ticket: "piào"
One way ticket: "dānchéng piào"
Round trip ticket: "wàngfǎn piào"
Platform: "dàntīng"
Exit: "chūkǒu"

When taking public transportation, it's essential to know the route number and the destination of the vehicle. You can ask for help by saying "qǐngwèn which means "excuse me" or "may I ask." For example, you can ask "qǐngwèn, zhè ge gōnggòng qìchē qù nǎlǐ?" which means "Excuse me, where does this bus go?"

Emergency Vocabulary

Although Taiwan is a relatively safe country, emergencies can happen anywhere and at any time. Here are some essential emergency vocabulary words to help you in case of an emergency:

Help!: "jiùmìng"
Police: "jǐngchá"
Ambulance: "jīhù chē"
Fire: "huǒ"
Hospital: "yīyuàn"

Doctor: "yīshēng"

Emergency: "jíjīn"

In case of an emergency, it's essential to call the appropriate emergency services. In Taiwan, you can dial 110 for the police, 119 for the fire department, and 120 for medical emergencies.

Knowing some basic phrases and vocabulary words can make your trip to Taiwan much more enjoyable and memorable. With this list of essential words and phrases related to basic communication, food and drink, transportation, and emergencies, you'll be able to navigate Taiwan with ease and communicate effectively with locals. Remember, the key to learning a new language is practice, so don't be afraid to try out your new vocabulary on your trip to Taiwan.

Taiwan Dos and Don'ts

Taiwan is a lovely island country in East Asia that is well-known for its thriving cities, gorgeous natural landscape, extensive cultural history, and delectable food. It is a well-known travel destination that draws millions of tourists each year from all around the globe. However, just like any other nation, Taiwan has its own set of traditions, conventions, and cultural norms that travelers should be aware of before making travel arrangements. I will go through the dos and don'ts that every traveler should be aware of before visiting Taiwan in this book.

Dos:

Observe local customs and traditions with respect: When visiting Taiwan, it is crucial to remember to uphold the nation's traditions and customs. The people of Taiwan are proud of their traditions and are heirs to a rich cultural legacy. Visitors should be aware of these customs and respect them by dressing appropriately, acting appropriately, and speaking appropriately. When entering someone is house, you should take off your shoes as a sign of respect. You should also avoid pointing with your finger and bow instead.

Although English is commonly spoken in Taiwan, it never hurts to know a few Mandarin words and phrases to help you get by. Learning some fundamental words and phrases like "hello," "thank you," and "excuse me" may help you get along well with the locals. As kind and hospitable as they are, Taiwanese people would appreciate your efforts to learn their language.

Try the local cuisine: Taiwanese food is renowned for its unique combination of flavors, fresh ingredients, and cooking methods. Taiwan has cuisine for every taste, from cheap meals to fine dining. Try some of the local specialties, such bubble tea, stinky tofu, and beef noodle soup. Taiwanese culture is heavily influenced by food, so experimenting with new cuisine is a great way to learn about how people live there.

Visit the night markets: Night markets are an important part of Taiwanese culture and should not be missed by visitors. These crowded markets provide a large selection of street food, beverages, and mementos in addition to activities like games and live music. Shilin Night Market in Taipei and Liuhe Night Market in Kaohsiung are two of Taiwan's most well-known night marketplaces. Prepare to immerse yourself in the colorful ambiance of the night markets by arriving hungry.

Consider Taiwan's wide and effective public transportation network, which includes buses, trains, and metro lines. Public transportation is not only inexpensive, but it is also a great way to see the island. Visitors should get an EasyCard, a smart card that can be loaded with money and used on all types of public transit. It is an easy and practical method to go about Taiwan.

Visit the temples: Taiwan is home to a variety of stunning temples, each with a distinctive architectural style and history. These temples serve as both houses of worship and significant historical sites. The most well-known temples, including Longshan Temple in Taipei and Fo Guang Shan in Kaohsiung, should be visited by tourists. But before entering the temple, guests must remember to dress modestly and take off their shoes.

Discover the great outdoors: From majestic mountains to immaculate beaches, Taiwan is famed for its magnificent natural landscape. Travelers should set aside some time to appreciate Taiwan's breathtaking scenery and the great outdoors. Taroko Gorge, Sun Moon Lake, and Kenting

National Park are a few of the top destinations. Additionally, visitors should remember to bring the proper clothes and equipment, as well as sunscreen and bug repellent.

Although Taiwan is a secure and hospitable country, tourists should nonetheless be aware of their surroundings, particularly in busy locations or popular tourist destinations. Since stealing and pickpocketing may occur everywhere, it is always preferable to be safe than sorry. In particular, visitors should be mindful of their possessions while in busy places like night markets and public transit. Keeping crucial papers, including passports and visas, in a safe location is also a smart idea.

In Taiwan, it is usual to remove your shoes before entering a person's house as well as certain establishments like temples and some restaurants. Following this tradition, visitors should take off their shoes before visiting these locations. Due to the fact that it prevents dirt and germs from being tracked inside, this is a symbol of respect and cleanliness.

Taiwan is a lovely nation with a rich natural history; please respect it. Visitors must be careful to respect the environment and take responsibility for keeping it safe. This include avoiding activities that affect the environment, staying on approved hiking paths, and not littering. Additionally, visitors should be aware of local laws governing recycling and garbage disposal.

Don'ts:

Though Taiwan is a developed nation with several credit card choices, cash is still king in many establishments. Travelers should always have some cash with them, particularly when visiting tiny businesses or night markets. It is usually preferable to be prepared since certain locations could not take credit cards.

Be quiet and respectful; Taiwanese people are often reserved and courteous, so tourists should aim to be the same. Loud or raucous behavior might be seen as impolite and disturbing in public. Visitors should be careful how they behave, particularly in peaceful areas like temples.

Keep your chopsticks from sticking up:
Chopsticks are seen to be unlucky when left in a bowl of rice, much like incense sticks at a funeral. Visitors should place their chopsticks on a chopstick rest, if one is offered,

or across the top of the bowl.

Do not disregard the traffic signals; Taiwanese traffic may be hectic and perplexing, particularly for foreigners who are unfamiliar with it. Visitors must closely observe the traffic signs and pedestrian crossings and adhere to their instructions. Following the laws and being safe is always preferable than breaking the law, which may lead to penalties or even accidents.

Respect the flag: Taiwan's national flag serves as a reminder of the country's pride and identity. It should not be disrespected or used as a prop by visitors. This includes walking on it, using it as a towel or napkin, or utilizing it in any disrespectful or improper way.

Do not underestimate Taiwan's weather; the subtropical island may experience intense heat and humidity throughout the summer. Visitors should be equipped with adequate clothes and sunscreen and not underestimate the weather. They should be wary of the typhoon season as well, which lasts from June to October and may bring about wind and rain storms.

Avoid being too blunt; Taiwanese people like to

communicate in an indirect, courteous manner. Visitors should make an effort to do the same and refrain from being very direct or aggressive. This entails speaking courteously and refraining from correcting or criticizing individuals in front of others.

Taiwan is a lovely, hospitable nation with a fascinating history and culture. By adhering to these dos and don'ts and being fully immersed in the culture, visitors may have an amazing experience. Visitors may have a safe and pleasurable journey to Taiwan by respecting local customs and traditions, sampling the food, going outside, and being aware of their surroundings.

Taiwan offers visitors a unique travel experience with its diverse range of attractions, from stunning beaches to towering mountains, vibrant night markets, and traditional festivals. This guide will guide you through a 15-day itinerary of the best places to visit and things to do in Taiwan.

Day 1: Taipei

Begin your journey in Taipei, the capital city of Taiwan. Taipei is a bustling metropolis with a mix of modern and traditional architecture, world-class museums, and fantastic cuisine. Start your day by visiting the iconic Taipei 101, one of the tallest buildings in the world. Take a ride to the top of the tower to enjoy the stunning panoramic views of the city.

Afterward, head to Chiang Kai-Shek Memorial Hall, a national monument built in memory of the former president of Taiwan. Here, you can witness the changing of the guard ceremony, a daily ritual performed by the military police.

In the afternoon, visit the National Palace Museum, which houses one of the world's largest collections of Chinese art and artifacts. The museum is home to over 700,000 pieces of art, including jade carvings, calligraphy, and ancient bronzes.

In the evening, explore the vibrant night markets of Taipei, such as Shilin Night Market or Raohe Night Market. These markets are famous for their street food, including stinky tofu, oyster omelets, and bubble tea.

Day 2: Taipei

On your second day in Taipei, visit the Longshan Temple, one of the oldest and most significant temples in Taiwan. The temple is dedicated to Guanyin, the goddess of mercy, and is an important center of worship for Taiwanese Buddhists and Taoists.

Afterward, head to Beitou, a district in northern Taipei famous for its hot springs. Here, you can soak in the natural hot springs and enjoy the stunning scenery of the surrounding mountains.

In the evening, head to Ximending, a bustling pedestrian area in Taipei's Wanhua district. Here, you can explore the vibrant nightlife of Taipei, with plenty of restaurants, bars, and nightclubs to choose from.

Day 3: Yilan

On your third day, leave Taipei and head to Yilan, a county in northeastern Taiwan famous for its natural beauty and hot springs. Start your day by visiting the National Center for Traditional Arts, a cultural center dedicated to preserving traditional Taiwanese art and crafts.

Afterward, head to Wufengchi Waterfall, a stunning waterfall located in the lush forests of Yilan. The waterfall is a popular spot for swimming and picnicking.

In the evening, relax in one of Yilan's hot springs, such as Jiaoxi Hot Springs or Toucheng Hot Springs. These hot springs are renowned for their healing properties and are a must-visit for any traveler to Taiwan.

Day 4: Taroko Gorge

On your fourth day, head to Taroko Gorge, a stunning natural wonder located on Taiwan's east coast. The gorge is over 19 kilometers long and is famous for its towering marble cliffs, crystal-clear streams, and breathtaking waterfalls.

Start your day by visiting the Shakadang Trail, a scenic

hiking trail that takes you through the gorge's stunning scenery. Along the way, you'll pass by the Shakadang River, one of the most beautiful rivers in Taiwan.

In the afternoon, visit the Swallow Grotto Trail, a scenic trail that takes you through a narrow canyon with towering cliffs on either side. The trail is home to hundreds of swallows, and you can often see them darting through the canyon.

In the evening, head back to your hotel or find a local restaurant to enjoy some delicious Taiwanese cuisine. Taroko Gorge is known for its aboriginal culture, and you can find restaurants that serve traditional aboriginal dishes such as wild boar or bamboo rice.

Day 5: Taitung
On your fifth day, head to Taitung, a county located on the southeastern coast of Taiwan. Taitung is famous for its stunning natural beauty, including beaches, hot springs, and mountain ranges.

Start your day by visiting the Taitung Forest Park, a beautiful park with walking trails, gardens, and a lake. The park is home to over 2,000 species of plants and animals, including rare orchids and butterflies.

Afterward, head to the Beinan Cultural Park, a museum dedicated to the prehistoric culture of the Beinan people, who lived in Taiwan over 2,000 years ago. The museum features exhibits on Beinan artifacts, burial practices, and culture.

In the evening, head to the Taitung Night Market, one of the largest and most popular night markets in Taiwan. The market features a variety of food stalls, game booths, and souvenir shops, and is a great place to experience the local culture.

Day 6: Kenting

On your sixth day, head to Kenting, a national park located on the southern tip of Taiwan. Kenting is famous for its stunning beaches, clear waters, and coral reefs.

Start your day by visiting Kenting National Park, which covers over 33,000 hectares and includes a variety of natural habitats, including forests, grasslands, and coastal areas. The park is home to a wide range of wildlife, including monkeys, deer, and sea turtles.

Afterward, head to Kenting's famous night market, where you can sample a variety of Taiwanese street food, including grilled squid, fried chicken, and stinky tofu.

In the evening, head to one of Kenting's famous beaches, such as Nanwan Beach or Baishawan Beach. These beaches are popular spots for swimming, surfing, and snorkeling.

Day 7: Tainan

On your seventh day, head to Tainan, a city located on the southwestern coast of Taiwan. Tainan is known for its rich history and cultural heritage, with many temples, museums, and historical sites to visit.

Start your day by visiting Anping Old Fort, a historical fort built by the Dutch in the 17th century. The fort features exhibits on the history of Tainan and the Dutch colonization of Taiwan.

Afterward, head to Chimei Museum, a world-class museum featuring collections of Western art, musical instruments, and natural history specimens.

In the evening, head to Tainan's famous night markets, such

as Flower Night Market or Garden Night Market. These markets feature a variety of food stalls, game booths, and souvenir shops, and are a great place to experience the local culture.

Day 8: Kaohsiung

On your eighth day, head to Kaohsiung, Taiwan's second-largest city. Kaohsiung is a bustling city with a mix of modern and traditional architecture, world-class museums, and fantastic cuisine.

Start your day by visiting Fo Guang Shan Buddha Museum, one of the largest Buddhist museums in the world. The museum features exhibits on Buddhist art, culture, and philosophy, and includes a giant Buddha statue that stands over 100 meters tall.

Afterward, head to the Liuhe Night Market, one of Kaohsiung's most famous night markets. The market features a variety of food stalls, game booths, and souvenir shops, and is a great place to experience the local culture.

In the evening, head to the Love River, a famous river in Kaohsiung that is illuminated by colorful lights at night. You can take a boat ride along the river and enjoy the beautiful views of the city.

Day 9: Penghu

On your ninth day, take a short flight to Penghu, a group of islands located in the Taiwan Strait. Penghu is famous for its pristine beaches, crystal-clear waters, and traditional architecture.

Start your day by visiting the Penghu Whale Cave, a natural cave formed by volcanic activity. The cave features stalactites and stalagmites that have been shaped by water and wind over thousands of years.

Afterward, head to the Penghu Great Bridge, a historic bridge that connects two of Penghu's main islands. The bridge is a popular spot for watching the sunset and taking photos.

In the evening, head to the Penghu Night Market, a lively market that features a variety of food stalls, game booths, and souvenir shops. Be sure to try some of the local seafood, such as grilled squid or fried fish cakes.

Day 10: Sun Moon Lake

On your tenth day, head to Sun Moon Lake, a picturesque

lake located in central Taiwan. Sun Moon Lake is famous for its stunning views of the surrounding mountains and its crystal-clear waters.

Start your day by taking a boat ride around the lake, which offers beautiful views of the lake and its surrounding scenery. You can also visit some of the temples and shrines located around the lake, such as Wenwu Temple or Xuanzang Temple.

Afterward, head to the Sun Moon Lake Ropeway, a cable car that takes you up to the Formosan Aboriginal Culture Village, a theme park that features exhibits on Taiwan's aboriginal culture and traditions.

In the evening, head to one of the restaurants near the lake and enjoy some of the local cuisine, such as grilled tilapia or aboriginal-style dishes.

Day 11: Nantou

On your eleventh day, head to Nantou, a county located in central Taiwan. Nantou is known for its stunning natural beauty, including mountains, forests, and lakes.

Start your day by visiting the Xitou Forest Recreation Area, a beautiful park with walking trails, gardens, and a lake. The park is home to over 1,000 species of plants and animals, including rare birds and butterflies.

Afterward, head to the Puli Brewery, a brewery that produces some of Taiwan's most famous wines and spirits. The brewery offers tours and tastings, where you can sample some of their delicious products.

In the evening, head to the Fengjia Night Market, one of the largest and most popular night markets in Taiwan. The market features a variety of food stalls, game booths, and souvenir shops, and is a great place to experience the local culture.

Day 12: Hualien
On your twelfth day, head back to Hualien, where you can explore some of the city's other attractions that you may have missed on your first visit.

Start your day by visiting the Chihsing Tan Scenic Area, a beautiful beach with black sand and stunning views of the Pacific Ocean. You can also visit the Hualien Ocean Park, an aquarium that features a variety of marine life from around the world.

Afterward, head to the Hualien Cultural Creative Industries Park, a park that features exhibitions on Taiwan's cultural heritage and traditional crafts. The park also has a variety of shops and restaurants where you can buy souvenirs and sample some of the local cuisine.

In the evening, head to the Dongdamen Night Market, one of Hualien's most famous night markets. The market features a variety of food stalls, game booths, and souvenir shops, and is a great place to experience the local culture.

Day 13: Taipei (Second Visit)
On your thirteenth day, return to Taipei for your final few days in Taiwan. Since you've already seen some of the city's main attractions, you can spend the day exploring some of the lesser-known areas of the city.

Start your day by visiting the National Taiwan Museum, the oldest museum in Taiwan. The museum features exhibits on Taiwan's history, culture, and natural environment.

Afterward, head to the Huashan 1914 Creative Park, a park that features exhibitions on Taiwan's cultural heritage and contemporary art. The park also has a variety of shops and restaurants where you can buy souvenirs and sample some of the local cuisine.

In the evening, head to the Raohe Night Market, one of Taipei's most famous night markets. The market features a variety of food stalls, game booths, and souvenir shops, and is a great place to experience the local culture.

Day 14: Yilan

On your fourteenth day, take a day trip to Yilan, a county located in northeastern Taiwan. Yilan is known for its natural hot springs, scenic mountains, and traditional aboriginal culture.

Start your day by visiting the Wufengchi Waterfall, a stunning waterfall located in the midst of a lush forest. You can also visit the Jiaoxi Hot Springs, where you can soak in the natural hot springs and relax in the midst of the beautiful scenery.

Afterward, head to the Yilan Traditional Art Center, a center that features exhibitions on Taiwan's traditional arts and crafts. The center also has a variety of shops and restaurants where you can buy souvenirs and sample some of the local cuisine.

In the evening, head to the Luodong Night Market, one of the largest and most popular night markets in Taiwan. The market features a variety of food stalls, game booths, and souvenir shops, and is a great place to experience the local culture.

Day 15: Taipei (Final Day)
On your final day in Taiwan, take some time to explore any areas of Taipei that you may have missed during your earlier visits.

Start your day by visiting the Taipei 101, the tallest building in Taiwan and one of the tallest buildings in the world. You can take the high-speed elevator to the observation deck on the 89th floor, where you can enjoy stunning views of the city.

Afterward, head to the Chiang Kai-shek Memorial Hall, a monument to the former president of Taiwan. The memorial hall features beautiful gardens, fountains, and a museum that showcases the life and legacy of Chiang Kai-shek.

In the evening, head to the Shilin Night Market, one of the most famous and popular night markets in Taiwan. The market features a variety of food stalls, game booths, and souvenir shops, and is a great place to experience the local culture.

Taiwan is a beautiful country with a rich cultural heritage and stunning natural scenery. With this 15-day itinerary, you can experience some of Taiwan's most famous attractions, as well as explore some of the lesser-known areas of the country. From Taipei's bustling night markets to Sun Moon Lake's peaceful surroundings, there is something for everyone in Taiwan. So pack your bags and get ready for an unforgettable adventure in one of Asia's most exciting destinations!

Conclusion

Taiwan is a fantastic place for tourists seeking a distinctive and memorable experience. Visitors are bound to be enthralled and inspired by the island nation's colorful fusion of cultures, history, and natural beauty.

Taiwan has a lot to offer, whether you want to experience pulsating metropolis or spend time in the outdoors. The island is home to an astounding variety of natural treasures that are guaranteed to wow you, from the towering peaks of Taroko Gorge to the gorgeous beaches of Kenting.

Taiwan has great cultural value in addition to its natural beauty. The vibrant night markets in Taipei and the elaborate temples that dot the island's landscape are just two examples of how rich the island's history and customs are. And its cuisine is well-known across the globe, with a variety and taste that will satisfy even the most discriminating palette.

One of the most appealing aspects of Taiwan is its people. One of the kindest and most hospitable individuals you'll ever meet is a Taiwanese person, and they absolutely excel at hospitality. No matter where you choose to stay—a hotel or a local family's home—you can count on receiving courteous service.

The country of Taiwan also has a cutting-edge, effective infrastructure. With an extensive network of high-speed trains, buses, and taxis, the island has one of the greatest transportation systems in the whole world, making travelling about a snap. Taiwan is also a highly safe tourist destination because to its first-quality healthcare system and low crime rate.

Overall, Taiwan is a place that every visitor should include on their bucket list. The island provides a unique experience that will leave you with memories that will last a lifetime, from its breathtaking natural scenery to its rich cultural legacy.

If you want to get the most out of your vacation to Taiwan, be sure to conduct your study in advance. Take advantage of the many excursions and experiences that are offered, including bicycle excursions, gastronomy tours, and cultural encounters.

Also, remember to dress appropriately for the weather! Depending on the time of year and location, Taiwan's climate may vary dramatically, so be sure to check the weather before you go and prepare appropriately.

Finally, once you are in Taiwan, remember to slow down and soak in the beauty and diversity of this amazing place. There's something wonderful about this island that is certain to captivate your heart and leave you wanting more, whether you're wandering through the busy streets of Taipei or climbing through the beautiful woods of Taroko Gorge.

Taiwan is a wonderful travel destination with a distinctive fusion of stunning natural scenery, a vibrant culture, and friendly locals. Everyone may find something to enjoy in Taiwan, whether they are an adventurous tourist or a history enthusiast. So why not start making travel arrangements right away and experience the magic of this amazing island nation for yourself?

Printed in Poland
by Amazon Fulfillment
Poland Sp. z o.o., Wrocław

22867659R00087